CHESAPEAKE CONFLICT
The Troublesome Early Days
of Maryland

Gene Williamson

HERITAGE BOOKS
2008

HERITAGE BOOKS

AN IMPRINT OF HERITAGE BOOKS, INC.

Books, CDs, and more—Worldwide

For our listing of thousands of titles see our website
at
www.HeritageBooks.com

Published 2008 by
HERITAGE BOOKS, INC.
Publishing Division
100 Railroad Ave. #104
Westminster, Maryland 21157

Copyright © 1995 Gene Williamson

Other books by the author:
Of The Sea and Skies: Historic Hampton and Its Times
Guns On The Chesapeake: The Winning Of America's Independence

International Standard Book Numbers
Paperbound: 978-0-7884-0330-9
Clothbound: 978-0-7884-7034-9

To Nancy with love.

Maryland's troubles began before there was a Maryland—in 1621, the year William Claiborne of England arrived in Virginia. Soon he discovered, purchased, named, and settled Kent Island in upper Chesapeake Bay. It led to the first serious boundary controversy in America when later Lord Baltimore's province was carved out of the territory originally granted to Virginia. This historic dispute, primarily between the parliamentarian Claiborne and the royalist Baltimore, was a colonial episode in the English Civil War and involved the first naval conflict in American waters. Though Parliament's overthrow of Charles I and the English monarchy in 1649 was a victory for Claiborne, resolution of the war in England and recognition of Charles II in 1660 restored Maryland to the Baltimore family.

CONTENTS

Acknowledgements

I am indebted to a number of individuals who encouraged me in the writing of this book but to none more than my sister Esther Kennedy who spent many hours assisting me in the research. I am grateful for the help I received at the public libraries in Hampton, Virginia, Baltimore and Kent Island, Maryland, Cape May County, New Jersey, the library research facility at Virginia's Christopher Newport University, the Maryland Archives, and the many excellent source materials listed in the bibliography. I also wish to express my appreciation to Mrs. Joseph E. Johnson who heads up the Claiborne Clan organization and publishes a newsletter for the descendants of the William Claiborne who figures so prominently in this book. Finally, I am indebted to Roxanne Carlson of Heritage Books for her editing skills and professionalism in preparing my manuscript for publication.

INTRODUCTION

" ... a royal pain in the breeches ... "

To the English in the early seventeenth century, America was Virginia, stretching from the Spanish missions on the Florida peninsula to the French trading posts in the St. Lawrence Valley. Of course, the Spanish claimed priority because they had explored the Chesapeake Bay and other regions along the Atlantic seaboard as early as 1529; the French could base their precedence on explorations in 1535 when their navigators named the St. Lawrence River. The English were not impressed; they traced their claims to the North American expeditions of John Cabot who had been commissioned by Henry VII in 1497 to find a northwest trade route to the Orient. No serious attention was given to claims of the native Americans (erroneously called Indians when Columbus thought he found India in the Caribbean); in European eyes they were infidels and savages who lived "in Darkness and miserable Ignorance of the True Knowledge and Worship of God."

In the 1580s Sir Walter Raleigh made a series of unsuccessful attempts to establish a Virginia colony in America, and never lost faith that he would "yet see it an English nation." But following the failure of Raleigh's fourth expedition in 1587, England's interest in colonizing America was not revived until the nation was confronted by such economic concerns as the overpopulation of its cities, the need for precious metals to replenish a treasury depleted by war, the desire to find a reliable source for the goods it was forced to buy elsewhere, and the lack of stable markets for its own products. It was financial self-interest that drove the early colonists, not some glorious adventure or nationalistic zeal to expand the empire. Despite the announced mission of converting heathens to *Protestant* Christianity, America was settled for profit, and more often than not England's hero was the self-made man of trade. As Linda Colley put it, trade was the nation's "muscle and soul ... the source of its greatness and the nursery of patriots."

England's first successful settlement of America was set in motion at the time its commerce was beginning to mature. In April 1606,

James I approved a petition by "certaine of the Nobilitie, Gentry, and Marchants" to form the London and Plymouth Companies. These joint-stock ventures were granted rights to establish two colonies on the Atlantic coast of North America. The Plymouth Company was to receive northern Virginia, roughly from today's Maine to the Hudson River, and the London Company would control southern Virginia, from New York to present-day South Carolina. Neither was to settle within one hundred miles of the other. In time the name Virginia was appropriated by the southern colony and the northern was called New England.

Initial attempts by the Plymouth Company failed and the enterprise was abandoned, not to be revived until the Pilgrims undertook "for the glorie of God, and the advancemente of the Christian faith, and honour of our King and Countrie, a voyage to plant the first colonie in the Northerne parts of Virginia." They had planned to set up a fishing village on the Hudson but were lost in a storm and landed at Cape Cod on November 9, 1620.

Meanwhile, the London Company equipped a fleet of three tiny merchant ships under the command of Christopher Newport: the flagship *Susan Constant*, the *Godspeed*, and the *Discovery*. As the ships left England on December 20, 1606, their complement included more than a hundred passengers, all of whom were company employees hired to search for gold and other precious metals and to establish trade with the Indians. These settlers were recruited from all levels of English life: many were sons of nobility; one a self-styled soldier of fortune; the remainder included a clergyman, blacksmith, barber, surgeon, mason, tailor, carpenters and bricklayers, a few soldiers, a sailor, and several small boys. None were prepared for the rigors of the American wilderness; all were lucky to survive the voyage. Sharing cramped quarters with swine, cattle, horses, and baggage, they had to endure months of treacherous seas, sickness, and threats of mutiny.

In April 1607 heavy winds drove the ships through the Virginia capes into Chesapeake Bay; the capes were named after the king's sons, Charles and Henry. That night, aboard the *Susan Constant*, Christopher Newport opened a sealed box containing the company's instructions for setting up the colony and a roster of the men who would serve as the colony's officials; the list included Captain John Smith who, for a brief period, would be forced to assume the dictator's role to maintain discipline.

While surveying the lower bay for a suitable location, the English anchored on April 30 near a sandy point they named Point Comfort, where Newport and several others rowed ashore, to be greeted by a friendly group of Indians who called their village Kecoughtan (present-day Hampton). The English stayed at the village long enough to see that it was a productive community of domelike wigwams located on some three thousand acres of cleared land. There men, camouflaged in skins, stalked deer and other game, and painted women gathered fruits and tended small plots of corn, squash, and beans. The village was surrounded by waterways teeming with fish, mudbanks abundant with clams, and in the bay a constant supply of oysters and crabs.

Early in May the three ships departed Kecoughtan, sailed away from the bay and up a wide river until they reached a narrow point of land where the English established their first permanent colony. They called it Jamestown in honor of James I, though the site's official designation was "London's Plantation in the Southern part of Virginia." It was not long before the English realized they had settled on pitch and tar swamps that were unhealthy, unproductive, and accessible to hostile Indian raids and looting. Within seven months, famine and disease reduced the original number of settlers to thirty-two. New settlers would continue to arrive, but they also would lack the training and the discipline to adjust to the harsh conditions. With their time and labor consumed by the quest for treasure, they were forced to plunder the Indian villages for food; and still the only treasure the company ships took back to England was "gilded durt."

In 1609 the London enterprise was rechartered and renamed the Virginia Company. Through the new charter, the impoverished colony acquired new boundaries two hundred miles north and south of Point Comfort and "from Sea to Sea," more than five hundred new settlers (of whom one hundred were women), and a new governor, Thomas West, Lord Delawarr, who arrived just in time to rescue Jamestown when it was about to be abandoned by a handful of settlers who had survived on "doggs, catts, ratts, and myce" during a period defined as *the starving time*. Under this charter, Virginians were entitled to "the rights of natural subjects of the Crown" but these were paper rights only. Still governed by a London council, the settlers lived under martial law, had no voice in their own affairs, possessed no property; they were the instruments of London commercial interests who exercised their authority through a company-appointed governor.

Lacking a forum to air their grievances, the settlers resorted to bitter quarrels that bordered on rebellion. The London response in 1612 was to grant yet another charter, shifting control of the colony from the council to the stockholders. Unfortunately, it was the conservative wing of the stockholders that initially seized the leadership and nothing changed to improve the lot of the settlers. How to improve company profits was the first priority.

By 1616 the Virginia Company had enacted measures to make the colony self-sustaining, so that it could provide the products that England was forced to buy at exorbitant prices from other nations and to serve as a market for English goods. The colonists, having given up hope of finding "the Pearle and Gold" promised in 1606 by Michael Drayton in his ode *To the Virginia Voyage*, began pursuing other means of creating profits for the company. Initial endeavors included glass production, iron making, lumbering, barrel making, and shipbuilding. Pitch, tar, timber, sassafras, and other natural products were loaded aboard ships returning to England. Virginia's chief source of revenue was the "stinking, nauseous, unpalatable weed" despised by James I, who had tried to pressure the colony to switch from tobacco and "use all possible diligence in breeding Silkewormes." But the king's plan was ignored as soon as John Rolfe abandoned the native plant for the seeds of a large leaf tobacco grown in the West Indies. When his experiments led to a crop that was tastier and milder with a more pleasing aroma, the exports to England increased from twenty-three hundred pounds in 1615 to more than forty thousand pounds in 1619. Tobacco, in Virginia, was like money, and the crop's profitability accelerated the arrival of new colonists, extending the settlement along the James and other major rivers, where the European ships discharged their wares and loaded tobacco at the wharves of the new plantations.

Thus the opportunity to own and cultivate land became a major inducement in recruiting settlers. In 1618, under the liberal and energetic leadership of London businessman Sir Edwin Sandys, the Virginia Company offered every Englishman the opportunity to take to the colony at least 250 people at his own expense, for which he received a tract of 1,250 acres or more, "confirmed as an estate of inheritance to him and his heyers forever." These tracts, known as hundreds, were the foundation of Virginia's plantation aristocracy.

F. J. Turner, in *The Frontier in American History*, wrote that American democracy was not carried to Virginia but was developed there under the demands of frontier conditions and the policies of a commercial company which held that everyone contributing to the success of the colony was "entitled to a dividend out of a common stock of land." Virginia was "in her origin a true Commonwealth," wrote Fairfax Harrison. Every new arrival "was taught that he was, by the mere fact of immigration, vested with a reserved legal right sooner or later to carve an individual holding out of [Virginia's] inexhaustible abundance of land." This fundamental "right" remained even after James I revoked the Virginia Company's charter in 1624 and made Virginia the first crown colony. And it would spread to the other colonies.

Thus, in the eloquence of Stephen Vincent Benet, there emerged from the transplanted English a new breed, the American breed:

And those who came were resolved to be Englishmen,
Gone to the World's end, but English every one,
And they ate the white-corn kernels, parched in the sun,
And they knew it not, but they'd not be English again.

Also on the agenda of Sir Edwin Sandys was the creation of a *self-governing* colony. Within the Virginia Company, he was a leader of the populist contingent supporting Parliament's campaign to end administrative abuse by checking the king's arbitrary power; and consequently he had enraged James I who urged the royalist bloc to elect a less progressive principal officer. But for now Sandys succeeded in advancing his aims for the colony, which included the abolishment of autocratic rule, encouragement of private property, and a "Great Charter of privileges, orders and laws." The latter was realized on June 30, 1619, when the first representative body in America assembled in the "Quire" loft of the Jamestown church, with twenty-two burgesses in attendance, two each from the towns, plantations, and hundreds (styled boroughs; hence, burgesses). The assembly officials were compensated with a pound of the king's hated tobacco from every Virginia male over the age of seventeen. A year later, in the company election demanded by the supporters of James I, the stockholders chose as their treasurer and new leader, Henry Wriothesly, third Earl of Southampton, a close friend of Sandys and a strong advocate of his liberal policies. The king's candidate received one vote.

At that time, a large segment of the English people were in the early stages of organized opposition to absolute rule of the monarchy. The mother country was dividing itself into two factions: the Court Party committed to the monarchy and the Country Party whose members believed that the people, through representatives, should have more active participation in government.

This was how things stood when William Claiborne, a member of the Country Party, sailed for Virginia in 1620 with Sir Francis Wyatt, the man instructed to oversee the constitutional reforms as Virginia's new governor. Claiborne was the colony's royal surveyor.

Claiborne would survey the Chesapeake and its many islands and tributaries as far north as the Susquehanna River; and though he would come to know the grandeur of this largest of North American bays, it would be left to future generations to learn that the Chesapeake was formed many millennia ago by glacial flooding, that its forty-six-hundred-mile shoreline was roamed by mastodons and camels, that crocodiles once swam its thirty-two hundred square miles of water, that its greatest depth is nearly two hundred feet, that four hundred streams feed its forty-eight main tributaries, of which nineteen are navigable.

Claiborne was preceded in his mission by Captain John Smith who had mapped the area's major waterways as early as 1608 in the hope of finding the mysterious northwest passage to "the Sea of China and the Indies," discovering gold or some other precious metal, and trading with the "salvages" for furs. An account of Smith's travels along the great rivers was written by the colony's first secretary, William Strachey, and summarized in my book, *Of the Sea and Skies*:

> "On the west side of the bay were 5 faire and delightful navigable rivers." The first, which flowed into the bay near Kecoughtan, was called Powhatan, "according to the name of a principall country that lyeth upon the head of yt." The English first named it King's River, and later the James. Strachey said it "falleth from rocks far west, in a country inhabited by a nation ... they call Monacan. In the furthest place that hath been diligently observed, are falls, rocks, showlds, etc." Above the falls, the James was fed by "the pleasant river of Appamatuck" and "two rivers of Quiyoughcohanock ... wherein falleth three or four pretty brookes and creeks, that half entrench the inhabitants of Warroskoyack; the river of Nandsamund, and lastly, the brooke of Chesapeak [today's Elizabeth River at Norfolk]." North of the James was Chicahamania, "the back river of James Towne; another by the Cedar Isle, wherein are great stoore of goodly oysters; then a convenient harbour for crayes, frygatts, or fisher-boates, at Kecoughtan, [which] turneth ytself into baies, coves, and creeks,

that the place is made very pleasant thereby to inhabite." It was noted that most of the "by rivers" gave their names to the nations or families that lived along their banks.

"Fourteen miles northward from the river Powhatan," wrote Strachey, "is the river Pamunck, which we call the Prince's River." Later named the York, the river "divideth ytself, at Cinquoteck, into two gallant braunches: on the south braunch enhabite the people of Youghtamund; on the north braunch, Mattapament. On the north side of this river is Kiskiack; these, as also Appamatuck, Orapaks, Arrohatack, and Powhatan, are the great king's inheritance, chief alliance, and inhabitaunce. Upon Youghtamund is the seate of Powhatan's three brethren, whome, we learn, are successively to govern after Powhatan, in the same dominions which Powhatan, by right of birth, as the elder brother, now holdes. The rest of the countryes under his command, are ... his conquests."

The third navigable river which "the Naturalls of old" called Opiscatumeck was of late the Tappahannock. The English named it Queen's River, then Rappahannock. "The fourth river," wrote Strachey, "is called Patawomeck, and we call it Elizabeth River." It was to become again the Potomac. "The fifth river is called Pawtuxunt, and is of less proportion than the rest. Upon this river dwell the people called Aquintanacsuck, Pawtuxunt, and Mattapament." Thirty leagues to the north was a river inhabited by a people called "Sasquehanoughs."

Commenting on Smith's mapping of the Chesapeake regions, the historian William R. Robertson wrote in 1777: "So full and exact are his accounts of that large portion of Virginia and Maryland that after the progress of information and research for a century and a half, his map exhibits no inaccurate view of both countries."

Legend has it that Claiborne met the captain in 1620 when he lived in London, and that Smith encouraged him to seek his fortune in the Virginia colony. In so doing, Claiborne's life in Virginia, like Smith's, was clouded in controversy—conflicts that had to do with boundaries and territorial rights, which in the development of English America were loosely defined and frequently ignored. For many years Claiborne waged his own personal war against Maryland authorities to defend and then recover an island in the upper bay which he believed was rightfully his. That island (and others) had been confiscated by Cecil Calvert, second Lord Baltimore, the man rewarded for his loyalty to the king with full proprietary rights to the Virginia territory located north of the Potomac River. The Claiborne-Baltimore conflict, which evolved into a colonial extension of the civil uprising in England, dominated events and issues which helped to shape the Maryland colony.

Though Claiborne lost the war, he remained true to his motto, *Adversity no Disgrace*, and eventually accumulated his fortune. His life in America, spanning fifty-six years, could have been perhaps idyllic had it not been for his obsession to rule a far-flung fur trading empire from a small island in the upper Chesapeake. Both praised and damned, he was treated with comic disdain in Fodor's *Chesapeake*: "Trader Claiborne stuck around long enough to become a royal pain in the breeches to his king and to Lord Baltimore, but that's another story."

It is in fact the story of early Maryland.

CHESAPEAKE COUNTRY
(Map Legend)

1 Chesapeake Bay	16 Mattaponi River
2 James River	17 St. Mary's
3 York River	18 Piscataway
4 Rappahannock River	19 Anacostan
5 Potomac River	20 Kent Island
6 Patuxent River	21 Choptank River
7 Susquehanna River	22 Popeley's Island
8 Palmer's Island	23 Claiborne Island
9 Pocomoke River	24 Jamestown
10 Pocomoke Sound	25 Delaware Bay
11 Cape Charles	26 Romancoke
12 Cape Henry	27 Eastern Shore
13 Kecoughtan	28 Providence
14 Accomac	29 Atlantic Ocean
15 Pamunkey River	

William Claiborne
(1600-1677)

One

The Man From Kent
1600-1629

He influenced the development of two American colonies. This Virginian dominated the stage on which Maryland's early drama was played out. He was as famous (and infamous) in his day as just about any of the pioneering Americans. Yet today's historical texts rarely mention his name.

He was William Claiborne.

In his native England he was the son of a family schooled in commerce; and for more than half a century in his adopted Virginia, his actions were ruled by dreams of wealth and power built on the trading enterprise he battled to establish in Chesapeake Bay. By age twenty-five he had gained position and political clout through royal commissions; in his forties he was branded a "turncoat" when he supported Parliament in its opposition to the absolute rule of kings; in his sixties he was again favored by the crown.

According to more than one source, Claiborne was a self-made man of many facets: surveyor, fur trader, and planter; soldier and government official. Restless and acquisitive, he was a man of passion who was tenacious and sometimes violent in defense of his property and his rights. He was a hero to many, a pirate to others; "faithful to his friends and faithful to his enemies."

William's father, Thomas Cleyborne, like his grandfather, had been a county administrator and "merchant gentleman" with shipping interests in Norfolk County, England, before moving to Kent County in 1600. His various enterprises included trade in Icelandic fish and the manufacture of white salt. In 1598, Thomas married Sara Smyth James, the comely widow of a London brewer. By 1606 Sara had given birth to five children: Thomas, William, Sara, Katherine, and Blanche.

William was baptized in the Kent County parish of Crayford on April 10, 1600. Early accounts were mistaken in dating his birth to 1587 at Cliburn Hall in Westmoreland County, but it is generally accepted that he was related to the ancient Cliburn family and was descended from Rolf the Norseman who conquered Normandy in 911. Thus, with the blood of Vikings in his veins, he also could trace his lineage to the Norman duke who invaded England in 1066 and won the English crown, William the Conqueror.

According to one Claiborne descendant, the name is spelled at least thirty different ways and is often confused with Claybourne, Clayborne, Cleborne, Cleburne, Cliburne, Cliburn, and Clibon. The name is derived from the Anglo-Saxon *claeg*, sticky earth or clay, and *burne*, a stream; hence, claystream. It was not until William arrived in America that he changed the spelling from Cleyborne to Claiborne. The evidence appears in this facsimile of his signature on his petition to the king's commissioners in March 1677:

Ironically, the Fates that would ultimately smile on William were not so kind to Cliburn Hall. Nathaniel C. Hale noted that the English Civil War (1640-49) reduced the Cliburns "to tilling the soil over which their ancestors had held sway for five hundred years," while that same conflict "brought historic renown" to the "upstart colonial kinsman" whose immediate family "had never tasted the sweetly satisfying plums of lordship."

William was no son of aristocracy; he was a young, educated heir of commerce who would find it necessary one day to assume the role of warrior in hostilities with both the Indians and his countrymen.

Born into a mercantile tradition and growing up by the mouth of the Thames in one of England's major commercial centers, William was fascinated by the growth of maritime activity at a time when his country's ships were searching the seas for treasure and trade. From local merchants and other adventurers in Kent, he heard about the harsh conditions confronting the Virginia settlers—starvation, disease, Indian warfare—but he was longing to share in the incredible riches he had heard about—the gold and silver artifacts being shipped to Spain from the ancient cultures in Central and South America. William had been told about Virginia and the Chesapeake Bay trading possibilities by Captain John Smith, who apparently was so impressed by the youth that he bestowed the name "Claiborne Iles" on a small cluster of islands he spotted while surveying the New England coast for a combine of London merchants.

Highly intelligent and inquisitive, impatient to get on with his life, William entered Pembroke College, Cambridge, in 1617 when he was sixteen years of age. Hale described the Cambridge University of that period as "a veritable seminary of liberalism," and this environment must have had a strong influence on young William who adopted both the liberal leanings of the early Puritans and the populist politics of the Country Party. Thus he was an active supporter of Parliament in its struggle against the divine rule of James I, who had summed up his disdain for the House of Commons when he said, "I am obliged to put up with what I cannot get rid of." Though he tried.

William "proved to be a good scholar and ... a young person of accredited ability," wrote Clayton Torrence; for at the age of twenty he was selected by the Virginia Company to go to Jamestown as the colony's surveyor. The company was then controlled by the liberal faction of stockholders headed by the Earl of Southampton, Sir Edwin Sandys, and Nicholas Ferrar who (like Sandys) was the son of a wealthy merchant.

Claiborne's appointment read as follows:

The Committee appoynted by the Preparative Courte to treat with Mr. Cleyborne (Commended and proposed for the Surveyors place) haveinge mett the next day and takinge into their considerations the allowances that a former Committee had thought fit to State that Office withall in respect of the service hee was to performe as well in generall as particular Surveys did agree for his Salary to allow him Thirty pounds per annum to be paid in two hundred waight of Tobacco or any other valuable Comoditie growinge in that Country and that hee shall have a convenyent howse provided at the Companies charge and Twenty pounds in hand to furnish him with Instruments and books fittinge for his Office which hee is to leave to his Successor. Butt for the matter of his dyett [board] which was formerly appoynted to be with the Governor findinge therein some difficultie and inconvenience they had in leive thereof thought fitt to allowe him the free transporte of a third person besides himselfe and his servant and have given him 200 Acres of Land of Olde

Adventure for an inheritance; And in case hee shall be supplyed in matter of Survey for any pryvate man his wages shall not exceed six shillings per diem besides his Lodginge and Dyette which he that employs him shall pay him for; The said allowance beinge now putt to the question this Court did ratifie and confirme And fyndinge Mr. Cleyborne contented to goe uppon the sayd conditions have accepted him to be surveyor for three years.

Of particular interest to William Claiborne, whose goals for the Virginia adventure extended beyond surveying to opening trade relations with the Indians, were company instructions to develop *general* surveys, including "a true Mapp and face of the whole country coasts Creeks rivers highe ground and Lowe ground etc," as well as surveys for the hundreds and plantations where the boundaries should "bee perfectlie sett forth from tyme to tyme [and] mayntayned to prevent thereby future differences that arise upon questions of possession." This latter instruction was intended, of course, "for the better sattisfaction of the planters whoe we have now sent and furnished out Mr. William Cleyborne gentleman, recommended unto us as very fitt in ye art of surveying."

In November 1620, Sir Francis Wyatt and his party sailed from England aboard the *George*, an armed ship of one hundred fifty tons, escorted by the eighty-ton *Charles*. Wyatt, newly appointed governor recommended by Southampton to administer the reforms spearheaded by Sandys, was great-grandson of Sir Thomas Wyatt, the famous Kentish poet and alleged lover of Anne Boleyn before she became the second queen of Henry VIII. The governor's party included Lady Wyatt; Sir Edwin's brother, the poet George Sandys whose translation of Ovid's *Metamorphoses* would become the first major literary work produced in America; Dr. John Pott, Physician to the Colony and expert "in Distillinge of waters"; Sir William Newce, who was commissioned to fortify Virginia "against all forraigne invasions"; the Reverend Haute Wyatt, the governor's brother and a Puritan sympathizer sent to minister to an Anglican colony; Captain George Thorpe, who would oversee the construction of a college at Henrico for educating the settlers' children and civilizing the children of the Indians; the new secretary of state, Christopher Davison; and Claiborne.

The William Claiborne who boarded the *George* was described as a young gentleman dressed in the latest London vogue: a "straight-waisted orange doublet with a lace neck-whisk ... dark breeches [that were] bagging wide above the knees ... pale colored boots, [one of which] was carefully turned down below the knee to expose a ribbon tied about a yellow stocking." A rapier hung from his sword belt, "and buckled to the same belt on the right side was a long, tapering Italian dagger, ornamented and tightly sheathed." On his head, he wore a "new beaver hat, with a tall tapering crown and feathers." In his traveling chest were Claiborne's books and surveying instruments; strapped to the chest was a "half suit of armor, a breast and back plate." He also had a pistol with a sack of shot and powder. Below, there were Claiborne's furniture and a supply of "trucking stuff" (baubles, rings, copper chains, hatchets, hoe heads) for trading with the Indians.

Portraits of William Claiborne reveal a short, handsome man whose defiance is seen in his challenging, deep-set eyes, broad brow, and firm mouth. His long thin face, adorned with a mustache and goatee, is framed in dark curls. To compensate for his short stature, wrote Hale, he mastered the skills of the swordsman, displaying such finesse "in the manipulation of his blade that few cared to risk a friendly match with him."

It was evident from the kind of men who sailed with Wyatt to Virginia, that the company under Southampton was determined to improve the return on its investment by strengthening the colony's leadership, morale, and resolve. Still, there were very few men of "birth and quallyty" who dared venture into the wilds of Virginia. Most of the early colonists who achieved prominence were men of humble origin who acquired political power or position through land holdings and the fortunes they made from tobacco. Their descendants would become the plantation aristocracy that ruled Virginia society in the next century.

William Claiborne was twenty-one years of age when the *George* and the *Charles* sailed through the Virginia capes into the lower Chesapeake on August 8, 1621, to be welcomed by the cannons of the Point Comfort fort guarding the entrance into the James River. The ships anchored while the new governor was rowed ashore to exchange greetings with the fort commander and to report that the voyage had been calm, without the loss of a single life among the two hundred passengers—a significant achievement in the seventeenth century, when death was not uncommon in the filthy holds of the small merchant vessels. Nor was death a stranger in the colony. In spite of the mass immigration to the colony in previous years—averaging a thousand settlers a year—the population stood at only twelve hundred when Claiborne arrived.

But on this warm August day as Virginia's new surveyor stood on the deck of the *George*, gazing at the site of an ancient Indian village near the mouth of majestic Chesapeake Bay, he decided that he had reached the Promised Land. Reality would not strike until the following year, when the Indian massacre of 1622 nearly wiped out the colony.

Claiborne had no sooner moved into the living quarters provided for him at Jamestown than he was actively engaged in carrying out the instructions addressed to the governor and his council:

> *Itt is our expresse will that the tenants belonging to every ofice be fixed to his certaine place upon the land sett out for itt, for which Mr. Cleyburne is Chosen to be our Surveyor, who att the Companies very great charge is sett out as by his condition of agreement you may perceive. Great hath beene the care of the Company to sattisfie your desires that they have spared for no paines nor charge: The Publique lands sett out, and that which belongs to publique persons; his next employment must bee to sett out lands belonging unto particular Plantations, and then that he exceed when he is employed by any private persons the rate of six shillings the day, which sum must be duly paid in good and valuable commodities.*

Surveying was by no means an exact science in the early seventeenth century, even for a man educated in the technicalities and supplied with the essential instruments. Though land in Virginia was synonymous with capital, prior to 1621 the men who calculated the boundaries were at best mapmakers who lacked the technical training and instruments to make accurate surveys. For Claiborne, it was not the large public lands that proved troublesome; it was the private land patents where the boundaries were frequently in dispute. When the arguments were minor, usually they could be settled by his surveys. Major differences were referred to the governor's council. In any case, as he traveled on his surveying assignments from one end of the colony to the other in the company of his trusted servant, he had the chance to become acquainted immediately with colonists in each of the settled areas. He learned of their insecurities about the legality of their land holdings, their ambitions, their problems of coping with a hostile wilderness. Like Captain John Smith before him, his travels brought him into contact with the various native tribes, from whom he learned hunting and fishing skills, food preparation techniques, health precautions—the kind of knowledge that would help him survive and prosper on his future trading expeditions. He found that the main reason so many of the original settlers failed was because, in their English arrogance, they refused to learn from the Indians. Early on, Smith had urged the company to "send but thirty carpenters, husbandmen, gardeners, fishermen, blacksmiths, masons, diggers of trees' roots, well provided, rather than one thousand of such as we have." Now Claiborne observed that the new settlers were better conditioned for the wilderness, in training and in attitude, for even in the outlying areas there was a steady growth in cultivated fields and frame dwellings; and he saw too that the company's insistence on sending more and more women was generating a feeling of family life and stability—and permanence. As Claiborne busied himself in establishing the limits for new land grants, changing titles or adjusting the many disputed claims, his survey fees increased considerably—with some official stimulus as seen in the minutes of the governor's council:

> *Thomas Sulley hath bargained and sold his six Acres of Lande in James City Islande to Sir George Yeardley knight together with the Patent thereof for ever, for which Sir George is to pay him one hundred pownd waight of the best marchantable Tobacco in good meale, if any come in or ells if meale come nott in in other good Commodities and to pay Mr. Cleybourne for makinge the Patent.*

Claiborne noticed something else when he visited Elizabeth City: the growing import of black Africans. The trade had started in 1619 when a Dutch ship docked at Point Comfort and discharged a cargo of "20 and odd Negroes" from the West Indies. Mostly male between the ages of fourteen and thirty, the blacks were admitted as bonded servants to take over the manual labor of the unskilled and "generally incompetent poor whites" who would gradually abandon the established settlements for the wilds—perhaps to push on, as they imagined, the few hundred miles beyond the hills and forests to the riches of the Indian Sea. As it turned out, they settled on the Virginia frontier and became the forefathers of the vanguard of America's western migration. In the meantime, of course, the blacks lost their indentured status in the slave system that was installed by Virginia planters to maintain their tobacco economy.

One thing that neither Claiborne nor the other colonists had noticed in early 1622 was the intense hostility seething within the local Indians. Their patronizing behavior had lulled the Virginians into thinking that all was well. In fact, one of the newcomers to Kecoughtan described that ancient town as "every way soe well disposed that in that place well governed men may enjoy their health and live as plentifully as in any part of England."

But all was not well.

Three thousand years before the English settled Jamestown, peoples speaking the Algonquian language and occupying a region north of the Great Lakes, fanned out to the Great Plains of the west, the woodlands east of the Appalachian Mountains, and as far south as the Outer Banks of North Carolina. Among the strongest of the Algonquian were the Delaware Indians, who lived mainly on the banks of the river separating Pennsylvania and New Jersey, and the Powhatan, who had migrated to the Chesapeake and Tidewater regions of southeastern Virginia. There were three Algonquian groups in the Maryland area: the Nanticoke on the Eastern Shore, the Piscataway to the west between the Potomac and the Chesapeake, and a scattering of Susquehannocks at the mouth of the river flowing into the upper bay from what is now Pennsylvania.

Powhatan was also the name that Captain John Smith applied to its chief, whose proper name was Wahunsonacock. Among the tribes inherited by Powhatan were the Arrohateck, Appamatuck, Mattaponi, Pamunkey, Orapaks, and Kiskiack. Two of his conquered tribes were the Kecoughtan and the Chesepian, for whom the great bay was named. It was Powhatan's daughter, Pocahontas, who supposedly saved Smith's life; and in 1613 her marriage to John Rolfe greatly strengthened the friendship between the Powhatan and the English. But five years later that friendship was endangered when the eighty-year-old chief died. He was succeeded by his brother Opechancanough, who had sworn to punish the English for plundering the Indian cornfields.

That punishment came at noon on Good Friday, March 22, 1622, wrote Charles Campbell, when Opechancanough's warriors, "rising suddenly and everywhere at the same time, butchered the colonists with their own implements, sparing neither age, nor sex, nor condition: and thus fell in a few hours three hundred and forty-nine men, women, and children." Among the slaughtered were John Rolfe, George Thorpe, who had befriended Opechancanough and condemned the colony for mistreating the Indians, and Henry Spilman, slain while attempting to trade with the Anacostian Indians near the site of today's Washington, D.C. In retaliation, the English almost exterminated the neighboring tribes and drove the survivors away from the major rivers, greatly extending the lands held and cultivated by the colonists.

Opechancanough, however, escaped to fight another day. As did William Claiborne.

In 1624, while serving as Governor Wyatt's military aide in a series of retaliatory raids against Opechancanough, Claiborne and his company of sixty men were confronted by an Indian force of some eight hundred bowmen. The objective of the colonists was to burn a large crop of standing corn, but the warriors of this particular tribe were more concerned about protecting their reputation (having boasted that one day they would destroy the English). The bows were no match for English guns. After two days the Indians were driven into the woods where they could only watch "while theire Corne was Cutt downe." Incredibly, no colonists were killed, though a number were hurt, including Claiborne whose arrow wound in the right thigh would bother him for the rest of his long life. Again the English were unable to capture the wily Opechancanough.

For his military exploits Claiborne was given two parcels of land which totaled seven hundred and fifty acres. This land, plus one hundred and fifty acres he obtained by patent, was located near the Southampton River on the site of the Kecoughtan Indian village seized by the English in 1610 and renamed Elizabeth City after the daughter of James I. Still referred to as Kecoughtan by most of the colonists, it was currently Virginia's largest settlement and also its major port and official destination of supplies sent from England. New arrivals would be temporarily quartered there so that "the wearisomeness of the sea may be refreshed in this pleasing parte of the countrie." Situated in an open area on a great harbor at the mouth of the Chesapeake, Kecoughtan had so many fine "baies, coves, and creeks," wrote Captain John Smith, "that the place is made very pleasant thereby to inhabite." He praised the "mildness of the air, the fertility of the soil, and the situation of the rivers ... so propitious to the use of man, as no place is more convenient for pleasure, profit, and man's sustenance under any latitude or climate." Its deep-water wharves facilitated the loading and unloading of the merchant ships from England and elsewhere.

Among Kecoughtan inhabitants at that time were Francis West, the younger brother of Lord Delawarr, Virginia's first governor; William Tucker, a member of the governor's council; the Reverend George Keith whose Elizabeth City descendant George Wythe would teach law to Thomas Jefferson and sign the Declaration of Independence; John and Ann Laydon whose eldest daughter was the first English child born in the colony; William Capp who in 1619 was a Kecoughtan representative in the first assembly and would be the first to develop a saltworks to preserve the colony's food supply; and John Nott, whose patent showed that he was the first to open "a howse of entertainment, whereby strangers and others may be well accommodated."

As soon as Claiborne had recovered from his wound, he left Jamestown to manage his land holdings in Elizabeth City. In doing so, he moved from a swampy land that would never be healthy or productive to a site protected by wide stretches of water that made it easy to spot the approach of an enemy fleet or sneak attack by the Indians. There near the fort at Point Comfort he would set up a base for his fur-trading venture in the upper bay and be within easy reach of his official duties in Jamestown.

The trade was important, but so was the land. He had learned and seen in England that, in terms of wealth, position, and power, men of the merchant class were usually no match for the landowners, who appreciated the value of commerce but nevertheless considered men of commerce beneath their status. England's officialdom almost invariably consisted of gentry who possessed large landed estates, either inherited, appropriated, or received through the largess of the crown. Thus it must have occurred to Claiborne that it was not enough to run a successful trading post; it was imperative to his quest for wealth and power that he own and cultivate the land.

By the middle of the century, of course, the economic clout of the nation would be concentrated in the mercantile centers, which funded England's wars and expansion. England and its merchant class would become mutually beneficial. "Trade followed the flag," wrote Colley, "but it also helped to keep the flag flying."

In America in 1624, the English were new at the trading business, having been preceded by the French and the Spanish. For nearly a century, the French had been doing an active fur trade in the St. Lawrence Valley. The Spanish, from their base in Florida, had sailed into Chesapeake Bay and ventured as far north as the Potomac to barter for hides and skins. Meanwhile, England had been importing costly furs from Russia, Poland, and Flanders. And though Spain abandoned the Chesapeake after the English arrived, the French had expanded their trade activities. Moreover, Dutch traders now occupied the Hudson Valley and soon the Swedes would be trading for pelts on the banks of Delaware Bay.

Among the early English settlers unafraid to challenge the risks involved in the pursuit of beaver, otter, and other furs in the Potomac region was Henry Spilman who had lived with the Indians as a youth and learned their language and customs. Ultimately he obtained financial backing from English merchants and established his headquarters at Kecoughtan. In 1619, after gaining prominence as much for his knowledge of the Indians as his success as a fur trader, Spilman was hired by Governor Yeardley as his interpreter, an association that soon ended when Spilman was accused of inciting the Indians against the colony.

Another of the early bay traders who had good connections in England was Henry Fleet who was captured by the Indians in 1623 and lived with them for four years. He too learned the language and habits of the Indians so well that he was able to develop a sizable and profitable fur trade and leave his mark on the history of the regions surrounding Chesapeake Bay.

The only man who was to become more important as a Chesapeake fur trader than Fleet was William Claiborne. Their rivalry would lead Fleet to assist the Marylanders in their territorial dispute with Claiborne. But when Claiborne set up his Kecoughtan headquarters in 1624, he was unaware of any significant competition. Spilman, who would have been a neighbor, had been killed in the Indian massacre, and the captured Fleet was thought to be dead. One report did suggest "a miscellaneous lot of nearly one hundred fur traders altogether in and about the bay." So apparently the busy port was bustling with guides and interpreters ready to supply personal assistance, maps, and "trucking stuff" to newcomers who had been sent over by the company to trade with the Indians.

Just as Claiborne had settled in at Kecoughtan and acquired the boats, personnel, and supplies he would need for his trip up the Chesapeake, news arrived from England that would delay his plans and dramatically change his life. On May 24, 1624, King James revoked the company's charter and Virginia became the first crown colony. This was deemed the only solution to a situation in which the company expenditures were four times greater than the value of the Virginia exports. But with management distributed between the crown, the company in London, and the council in Virginia, the venture was destined to fail. Still, a majority of stockholders issued a statement which disagreed with the crown's indictment of company leadership and praised the Earl of Southampton, declaring that he had performed with "singular wisdome providence and care and much Noble paynes and industrie and with unquestionable integritie."

The company governor, Sir Francis Wyatt, was appointed royal governor in August. He and twelve councillors would rule the colony in the king's name. William Claiborne, just four years after his arrival in Virginia, was to be one of the councillors.

Fortunately for Virginians, James I died on March 27, 1625, thereby saving the colony's general assembly which James would not have approved now that Virginia was a crown colony. His successor, Charles I, though he believed as much as his father in the divine rights of monarchy, made no changes in Virginia's form of government. But to the despair of the planters, he also made no change in James's tobacco monopoly which channeled almost all of the profits from this "scurvy weede" into the pockets of the company members who had helped his father overthrow the company—including Privy Councillor George Calvert, first Lord Baltimore and the man who soon would be a bitter enemy of William Claiborne over territorial rights. Thus it was a bit of irony that Claiborne declared his support for a position favorable to the crown, one that would make tobacco the personal monopoly of Charles I, whose commissioners would set the price, the rate for freight, the customs, and the quantity that could be exported from Virginia. Claiborne saw this as a compromise that might somehow offer protection to the planters and clearly put himself in good stead with Charles I, by providing the king with a bargaining point for his acknowledgement of "the Grand Assembly of Virginia." As it turned out, Virginia planters emerged the winner because the assembly never did fully comply with the king's wish; instead it maintained a tight rein on the tobacco monopoly.

Compensating loyal courtiers with monopolies in the trade of particular commodities was a practice that James I had picked up from Elizabeth I in order to raise the money to meet government expenses and support his outlandish lifestyle. It was a system that indirectly taxed the poor because, in order to make a profit for the monopoly, it inevitably increased the cost of such items as salt, soap, spices, beer, bread, linen, and leather. Objections raised by the merchants and others with commercial interests were ignored by the king; and when opposed by the Puritan-dominated House of Commons he would invoke the "divine right of kings" and threaten to dismiss Parliament on the grounds that royal power was greater than the law of the land.

It was this lack of wisdom and diplomacy on the part of James I, and his successor Charles I, that would ultimately erupt in civil war.

William Claiborne received his personal reward for supporting the king on March 4, 1626. At that time Governor Wyatt was replaced by George Yeardley and the royal surveyor was elevated to the post second only to governor in political influence, secretary of state. Claiborne's appointment read as follows:

> *And forasmuch as the affairs of the said Colony and Plantation may necessarily require some person of quality and trust to be employed as Secretary for the writing and answering of such letters as shall be from time to time directed or sent from the said Governor and Council of the Colony aforesaid, our will and pleasure is, and we do by these presents nominate and assign you, the said William Clayborne to become Secretary of State, for the said Colony and Plantation of Virginia, residing in those parts.*

As secretary, Claiborne received "500 Acres of Land belonginge to that Office, and 20 Tennants to be planted thereuppon." Commonly called *The Secretary's Land*, it was located at Accomac near Cape Charles on the Eastern Shore. The Virginia council also allowed him an Indian servant who would prove to be useful as a guide in his fur trade. By court order the Indian servant was ruled an exception to the law declaring that "no man of what conditione soever within the lymitts of the first Suthern Colony of Virginia, shall make use of or ymploye any Indyan or keepe them after the same maner and forme, as he the said William Claybourne hath now projected and invented, uppon the forfecture of fower hundred pownde waight of Tobacco for every Indyan [he] shall soe kepe or make use of ..."

Thus, with the acquisition of the land at Accomac combined with his holdings in Elizabeth City, Claiborne, at age twenty-six, was rapidly becoming a man of substance. It would seem obvious that high office and membership on the governor's council strengthened his hand in obtaining a new commission from the council to generate trade with the Chesapeake Bay Indians.

On April 3, 1627, Claiborne was licensed by Yeardley to recruit a company of men to explore the rivers and creeks within the territory surrounding the bay, most of which was still unfamiliar country to the Virginia settlers, "and there to trade and truck with the Indians for furrs, skinns, corne, or any other commodities of what nature or qualitie soever they may be." A month later, he sailed from Kecoughtan in his shallop, which was easy to maneuver in shallow waterways and large enough to carry the cargo he hoped to bring back. Aware that the undertaking into strange waters was hazardous, he made certain that his men had "all necessaryes about them as gunnes or other Ammunition."

Following pretty much the route charted by Captain John Smith twenty years earlier, Claiborne headed first to his plantation at Accomac, then slipped in and out of the various creeks, taking his soundings and making sketches of the islands and coastline before crossing the bay and proceeding to the trade possibilities awaiting him in the upper Chesapeake. What captured his attention was an island he discovered beyond the Potomac, within close range of the Eastern Shore and opposite present-day Annapolis. This island, called Monoponson by the Indians, had been created when turbulent tides had cut a channel between the Eastern Shore and the bay.

It reminded Claiborne of his native Kent—but since it was not, by any stretch of the imagination, an island paradise, what was it that *really* attracted Claiborne? To J. Herbert Claiborne, it was his Viking heritage. This descendant suggested in 1917 that we look at the meaning of the word *viking*: "Most people look upon the word as implying a ruler of the sea, sea king or sea robber. The accent should be, not upon *king* but upon *vik*." He then noted that some etymologists believe "that *vik* is used in the sense of a *bay* or *harbor*." Thus: "A viking originally was a Norseman who sailed around in the bays and harbors, and made short sea trips." So it was probable "that the blood of the Vikings moved Claiborne to pick a piece of land somewhere by the sea. He must have loved the sea breezes of the Chesapeake, and in his nostrils was the breath of the north wind. He was truly a Viking since he spent a large part of his life sailing around in the bays and harbors of the Chesapeake. We see a distinct roving impulse here, and to some extent, a predatory one ... the moving impulse which drove him to this island and made him love it."

Of course, the attraction may have been more pragmatic. It may have been that once he learned the local Wicomesse and Matapeake Indians were eager to trade, he decided that this remote island would be an ideal place to build a plantation, with a manor house on the rise that looked out on the high grass and forests. The idea so pleased him that he thought he would call the island Kent and the plantation Crayford, after the parish in which he was baptized.

When he returned a year later to trade with the Wicomesse, Claiborne was impressed again with the island's strategic location for productive trade with the Indians on the upper bay, including those at the mouth of the Susquehanna River. The sight of the island's fertile fields confirmed his desire to build a great plantation which he could cultivate, stock with cattle, and settle with the families of men who shared his interest in maintaining a safe retreat that would not be overrun with other traders—and would serve as headquarters for a trading enterprise extending as far north as the Hudson River Valley.

News of Claiborne's arrival at Kent Island spread quickly to the surrounding villages, so that when he cautiously approached the nearby shores he would be greeted by "naked savages" whose strange noises and comic actions demonstrated their eagerness to trade furs for his axes, knives, and hatchets. Even with each side suspicious of the other, and each hoping to outsmart the other, these first expeditions

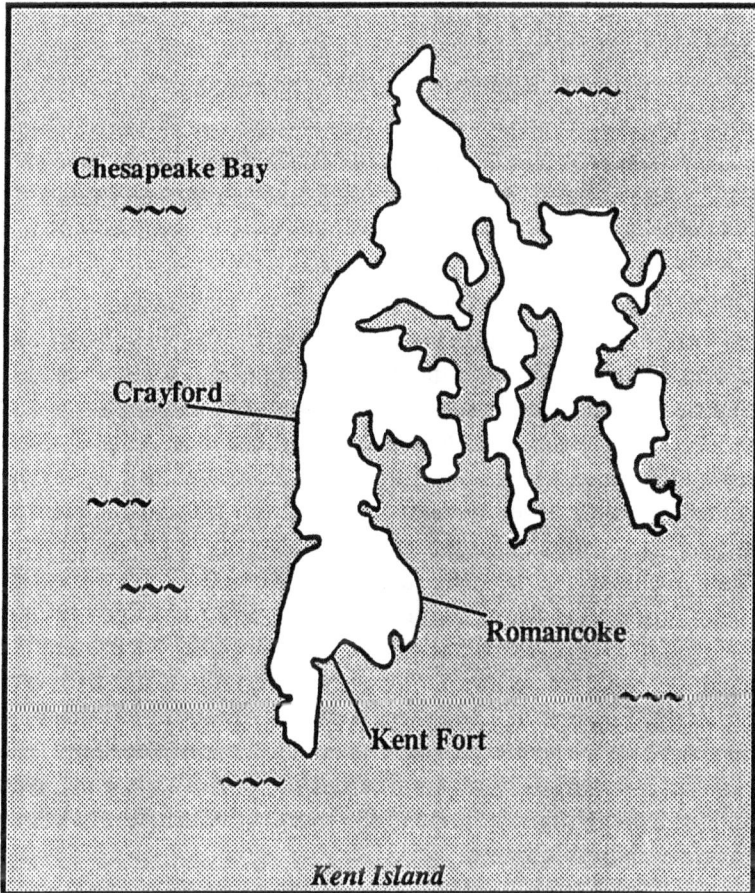

Chesapeake Bay

Crayford

Romancoke

Kent Fort

Kent Island

proved successful. Then, as his number of boats and trips up the bay increased, he sharpened his trading skills and established a reputation for fairness that would earn respect from the Indians wherever his boats landed.

In January 1629 Claiborne convinced his fellow councillors that his Chesapeake Bay venture would not only expand the colony's commercial activity to the Susquehanna River and beyond, but also would block encroachment by the Dutch and other European adventurers. Two months later he was commissioned by the acting governor, Dr. John Pott, to explore

> *the parts and territories of this colony situate and lying to the southwards of this place as also of some particular places to the northward and in the Bay of Chesepeiacke and greatly favoring the prosecution of such enterprises tendeth so much to the enlargement and welfare of this colony.*

Pott further granted Claiborne

> *full power and authority to govern correct and punishe such of his said Company as shall in any wise bee delinquent or obstinate to his authority and Command according to the Lawes and customes of the Seas, and as he in his best discretion shall think fitt life only excepted.*

Pott's commission laid the foundation for the trading post that Claiborne planned to establish at Kent Island.

It was on his 1629 voyage that Claiborne landed at a small island in the mouth of the Susquehanna and managed immediately to gain the friendship of the proud and fearsome Susquehannocks; he obviously inherited the trading genes of his merchant forebears, for it would be said that the bay Indians "would sooner trade with Captain Claiborne than with any other." This previously discovered island was described by an early observer as "halfe meade, halfe wood," on which there stands "a rock forty foot high, like a Tower, fit to be built on for a trading house for all the Indians of the Chispeak Gulf." A patent to the island had been granted by the Virginia Company in 1622 to Edward Palmer, a London art critic who planned to construct there "a Universitie" where students could "learne the art of payntinge." The grant was abandoned after Palmer's death in 1624, but the island continued to bear his name, and in 1631 would become part of William Claiborne's trading complex.

In 1629 William Claiborne commanded yet another military expedition in the ongoing retaliation against the Indians for their massacre of 1622. A renegade Indian guided him and his troops into the hostile Pamunkey country (at the head of the York River), where this time the English victory resulted in a peace treaty which, in effect, was a death sentence for the local Powhatans who continued to decrease in number, either from disease or the transformation of their ancestral lands into tobacco fields for the settlers. In a further attempt to beat the Powhatans into submission, Jamestown officials made it illegal to trade with any Indians except those on the distant Rappahannock and Potomac Rivers and those tribes across the bay on the Eastern Shore. Claiborne was rewarded, however, with five hundred pounds of tobacco and a large tract of land near the Pamunkey River. The Indian remained in his service as a guide and interpreter.

Claiborne's initial voyage up the Chesapeake "with a Companie of men in a shallop," and the trips he made in the following year through rivers, creeks, and havens along the upper bay, convinced him that trade with the Indians, if properly managed, would be more profitable than he had anticipated. Now, in 1629, with a vision projected beyond the Chesapeake to embrace the Delaware and Hudson Rivers as well as New England and Nova Scotia, he knew that the realization of this trading empire would depend upon his success in gaining financial interest in the enterprise.

To that end, he decided to sail to England.

Two

License to Trade
1630-1631

In an effort to revive the Virginia Company in 1629, a group of Virginia planters sided with a group of former stockholders. The coalition failed. Most colonists supported Virginia's status as a royal colony, despite the king's monopolies and other restrictions. But the full impact of crown pressure on the colony would not be felt until the 1630 arrival of the newly appointed governor, Sir John Harvey, a man called rapacious, haughty, and unfeeling by a later revolutionary from Virginia, John Marshall. Unjust and intolerant of the rights of others, he would ignore the council and enact his own laws without submitting them to the assembly. Harvey also had instructions from the royal commissioners to give away large tracts of land to friends of the crown—not just territory previously controlled by the company but lands belonging to individual colonists. Though no Virginian was more enraged by this practice than William Claiborne, his anger was temporarily mollified when Harvey renewed his license to explore Chesapeake Bay and other parts of the Virginia territory from the Potomac to the Hudson. But when Claiborne arrived in England seeking money for his Kent Island enterprise, he was told that he had violated the license by broadening his explorations to include direct participation in trade with the Indians. So the first thing he did after securing financial support was obtain a royal commission to trade "in any and all parts of North America not already pre-empted by monopolies."

The financing came from a partnership which Claiborne formed with William Cloberry, a wealthy London merchant who had friends among the king's advisors. Cloberry, aware of the trading possibilities in North America through an earlier affiliation with Canadian traders, was attracted to Kent Island's location. He agreed with Claiborne that the "very profitable and beneficiall trade that might bee had and made in the Bay of Chesopeake" could be expanded into the northern trading areas now dominated by the French, and that additional company profits could be achieved by supplying corn and other commodities to the settlements in New England and Nova Scotia.

The contract with Cloberry & Company stipulated that Cloberry would control two-sixths of the joint stock and that one-sixth would be held by Claiborne and each of the other three partners, Maurice Thompson, John Delabarr, and Simon Turgis. Claiborne was to be the company's representative in the colony and commander of the Kent Island trading post with complete management authority. His obligation was to "give unto his saide partners a juste and true accompte, soe farr as concerned the trade with the Indians, the transportation of corne and of all the profitts and benefitts anye wayes made by the saide joynte stock and otherwise."

To clarify the full extent of the company's trading rights, Cloberry said he would use his connections with the king's privy council to acquire Claiborne's patent under the "broad seale of England." The best he could do, however, was to promote "a trading commission under His Majesty's signet of Scotland." This was drawn by the Scottish secretary who bargained with Cloberry for a trade agreement between Virginia and Nova Scotia. The gist of the commission, as confirmed by Charles I on May 16, 1631, was that Claiborne and his associates were authorized to

> *freely without interruption from time to time to trade and traffique for corne furres or any other comodities whatsoever with their shipps men boates and merchaundizes in all seas coasts rivers creekes harbours lands and territories in neere or about these partes of America for which there is not allready a patent graunted to others for their sole trade ...*

The commission also provided that everyone, "and particularly our trusty and welbeloved Sir John Harvey Knight Governor and the rest of our councell of and for our Colonie of Virginia to permitt and suffer him and them ... to repaire and trade to and agen in all the aforesaid partes and places as they shall think fitt and their occasions shall require, without any stopp arrest search hindrance or molestation whatsoever as you and every one of you will answer the contrary for your perrills." Though Claiborne was not totally satisfied with the Scottish commission, it would gain the support of the Virginia government which he felt would protect him and his property in the upper Chesapeake from interlopers. As to Cloberry & Company, he felt that the profits he would earn from his share of the venture would soon remove any need of partners.

While in England, Claiborne visited his older brother Thomas who was a respectable but far from prosperous tradesman just outside London. Though the eagerness of Thomas to participate in the Virginia enterprise was dampened by his wife's opposition, the Reverend Richard James and Gertrude James, Claiborne's half-brother and half-sister, promised to make the trip within the year.

The thirty-year-old Claiborne also used this trip to look for a suitable wife, one who would be willing to endure the wilderness hardships with the prospect of sharing the fortune he expected to accumulate. He was delighted therefore when his brother introduced him to Elizabeth Butler (Boteler), just twenty and the youngest daughter in a family described as "bold and restless ... with a flare for trade and adventure." She was exactly what Claiborne had hoped for in a wife, and he began a campaign that would ultimately bring Elizabeth and her brother John to Virginia. Meantime, her oldest brother Thomas, and his wife Joan, accompanied Claiborne when he departed on May 28, 1631, aboard the *Africa*, a small merchant ship outfitted and manned by Cloberry & Company.

Two months later the *Africa* reached Virginia with twenty employees and a cargo of supplies and trading goods paid for by the company. The employees included an assistant for Claiborne, carpenters, laborers, farmers, house boy, and a "mayd servant to wash our linnen." Among the other passengers were several freemen (or freeholders) also employed for the Kent Island operation. "Wee arrived in Kecoughtan," Claiborne wrote, "where for the discharge of our shipp wee staied till the 11th of August."

It was about this time in 1631 that Claiborne, having added the title "justice" to his appointments, appeared at the hearings for a Kecoughtan resident, Goodwife Wright, who was accused of witchcraft. A neighbor claimed that she had put a spell on him, and now, after "a twelve months space [of] havinge very fayre game to shute at, he could never kill anything." Among other complaints, a farmer said that when he refused to sell her some chickens, she became so "sorely vexed" that the chickens died. It also was reported that once, when she was in a rage, she threatened to make a young maiden dance naked in public. In what sounds like a tale that could have been written two hundred years later by Nathaniel Hawthorne, her husband Goodman Wright said he had no knowledge of the strange things his wife was accused of, and apparently nothing came of the trial except to frighten Mrs. Wright into being more discreet in her incantations.

After leaving Kecoughtan, the *Africa* stopped at the Eastern Shore to recruit more freemen; their help was needed to maintain the trading post because the servants furnished by the company were too few in number. From there the ship continued up the bay to Kent Island, which Claiborne described as follows:

> *Entered upon the Isle of Kent, unplanted by any man. But possessed of the natives of that country, with about one hundred men and there contracted with the natives and bought their right, to hold of the Crown of England, to him and his Company and their heirs, and by force and virtue thereof William Claiborne and his Company stood seized of the said Island.*

The actual price that Claiborne paid for Kent Island in 1631 was twelve pounds sterling.

Immediately, Claiborne and his islanders set about building a fort, framed houses, huts, mills, storehouses, a shipyard, and a church. Soon the fertile fields were planted with corn and tobacco, orchards were cultivated, and livestock was grazing in the high grass. An inlet provided an excellent anchorage, and there was a protective cove large enough to hide two large ships. In the surrounding waters there was a variety of seafood and in the woods an abundance of game. Most important, in the swampy lowlands there were the beaver, otter, raccoon, muskrat, and other animals prized for their valuable furs. Claiborne had issued land grants under the Virginia charter, and soon Kent Island was occupied by more than one hundred colonists, many of them families. The island would be represented in the Virginia assembly by Claiborne's close friend, Nicholas Martiau.

The admission of Kent Island to representation in the general assembly reassured Claiborne that Virginia officials considered the upper Chesapeake region within their jurisdiction. So did recent legislation establishing inspection stations throughout the colony to regulate the planting and quality of Virginia tobacco; one of the stations was built next to Kecoughtan's Southampton River for the inhabitants of Elizabeth City, as well as those at Accomac and Kent Island.

Claiborne's island, only six square miles in area and more than a hundred miles from the lower settlements, appeared to be more permanent than did early Jamestown, which was almost deserted in 1609 because of famine, disease, and Indian raids.

By the time Kent Island was settled, Virginia was divided into four corporations, one of which was Elizabeth City. This was necessary to simplify administration because settlements now extended from Point Comfort along both sides of the James to the granite fall line near present-day Richmond, and across the bay at Accomac on the lower tip of the Eastern Shore peninsula. All were located on deep water with wharves to facilitate the loading and unloading of merchant vessels. Because there were no roads connecting the settlements, except the Indian trails, the only means of travel was by water. Not only was transportation faster and more convenient on the many waterways, it also was safer than following narrow trails through the woods where there was always the risk of ambush.

Because an outpost like Kent Island was isolated from other settlements, the islanders—as was true of colonists elsewhere—were defenseless without access to a boat. Thus it was not uncommon for boats as well as men to be pressed into action against hostile Indians, with the owners of the boats being compensated in tobacco.

Life in the Chesapeake and tidewater settlements depended upon all kinds of boats. The most popular were *pinnaces*, equipped with oars as well as sails, some large enough to cross the Atlantic as tenders for large vessels. The first pinnace constructed in America was built on Kent Island under Claiborne's supervision. Except for timber, almost everything required to build the boat (spikes, iron and brass plates, nails, joints, keel and rudder irons, ropes, tar, pitch) was purchased from the Kecoughtan supply depot. The *barque*, like the pinnace, was seaworthy and sometimes was used to transport supplies to New England and Canada.

Also built on Kent Island during Claiborne's command were the *shallops*, light open boats often used in loading tobacco hogsheads aboard larger vessels. *Sloops*, twice the size of the shallop, were sometimes used to transport people and freight beyond the Virginia capes. There also were *wherries, skiffs*, and *canoes*, small craft used primarily on the rivers and streams because they were unsteady in rough waters. Of the canoe, one visitor to the Chesapeake wrote:

> *The Indians call this watry Waggon*
> *Canoo, a Vessel some can brag on;*
> *Cut from a Poplar-Tree, or Pine,*
> *And fashioned like a Trough for Swine.*

Because there was always the danger the Indians would attack and slaughter the settlers on Kent Island, Claiborne defended the southern end of the island with a fort and several cannons. And whenever he and his men were on trading expeditions, times when they were most likely "to be sett uppon and taken by the Indians," they were heavily armed. Semmes wrote that on one occasion, when Claiborne was returning to Kent Island, his boat capsized near the Eastern Shore and, forced to go the rest of the way on foot, he was captured by the unfriendly Choptank Indians. Claiborne thought that he might have been killed had he not been rescued by a company of islanders despatched to search for him.

Yet, in spite of the dangers and hardships, the Kent Island trading post prospered, and Claiborne was hailed for his success in gaining "the sole trade & love of the Indians more than any other Englishman had." He often succeeded where others failed because he would adapt to the ways of a new culture, one with an expectation of strangers not so different from that of any other culture: for as the member of one of the upper Chesapeake tribes, a Wicomesse, advised the English:

> ... *since that you are here strangers, and come into our country, you should rather comform yourselves to the customs of our country, than impose yours upon us.*

Claiborne, unlike many of his countrymen, did not look down on the Indians as infidels to be converted or as simpletons to be cheated but rather as trading partners. To learn their customs he sent some of his islanders to live with the Susquehannocks, and there they were taught the value of the two kinds of Indian money, made from shellfish. Their *Wompompeag* was worth three times as much as their *Roanoake* and (reported Captain John Smith) both currencies caused "as much dissention among the Salvages as gold and silver among the Christians." The Susquehannocks, said one observer, were the "most Noble and Heroick Nation of Indians ... treading on the Earth with as much pride, contempt and disdain as can be imagined from a creature derived from the same mould and Earth." And because of their recent experience in trading with the Dutch along the Delaware, they had gained a reputation for craftiness. But they met their match in the man from Kent. It was said that "noe English that traded with the Indians ... gott soe much Beaver, with soe little Trucke & soe little supplies as Claiborne did." The result was that the beaver in the upper bay area were disappearing and the Susquehannocks had to hunt farther and farther inland to obtain their pelts.

The negotiating skills and grit that Claiborne had thus far demonstrated in his relations with the Indians would be put to a more difficult test in dealing with his own countrymen—notably Sir George Calvert who in August 1629 had asked Charles I for proprietary rights to "a precinct of land in Virginia." The request had been discouraged by the king and opposed by the Virginia council which managed to have the "hated papist" recalled to England when, because of his Catholicism, Calvert refused "to subscribe to the supreme authority of the English sovereign in all matters ecclesiastical and spiritual."

When Calvert returned to England to argue his case before the crown, the Virginia council sent Claiborne along to watch him and to block any actions that might endanger the council's authority. More important to Claiborne's acceptance of the mission was the need to prevent any encroachment on his Chesapeake Bay settlement. Virginia had already lost much of its southern territory to the "New Carolana" settlement of Sir Robert Heath and his associates. Now the most attractive option open to Calvert lay to the north, and it was known that he had surveyed the bay regions. Claiborne met with Francis West, who had served briefly as Virginia's governor, and others who were in England trying to restore the Virginia Company. Calvert, faced with their opposition and the king's pressure to remain in England for the good of his health, withdrew his petition for a Virginia land grant.

Meanwhile, with the winter approaching and Claiborne still in England, one hardship the Kent Island settlers had not anticipated was "a lamentable and fearfull fire." Describing the suddenness of the fire, one islander said that "not only the storehouses & goods belonging to the Jointstocke were burnt and consumed, but allsoe those of many of the Freemen which [had come to Kent Island] out of love to Claiborne." Most of the "trucking stuff" was destroyed, as well as furs obtained from the Indians.

On his return, Claiborne immediately despatched a letter to his London partners informing them of the loss and advising them of supplies that were urgently needed, particularly trading materials that would generate the greatest profit. While waiting to hear from London, Claiborne supplied many necessities for the island from his own goods and livestock in Kecoughtan. Though a number of servants had perished, he and the freemen managed to rebuild the storehouses and adjoining dwellings, tend the livestock, and clear the fields. Also at his own expense, Claiborne made several trips to Jamestown to replace the destroyed gunpowder and weapons, obtain clothing for the islanders and furnishings for the newly constructed houses—all of which burdened the income he received as secretary of state and as a member of the governor's council.

Claiborne's contract with Cloberry called for only one voyage, but now, in order to secure more financial aid, he was forced to extend his association with the company. Even so, the supplies sent to Kent Island were insufficient and the enterprise in 1631 survived only through Claiborne's dwindling resources and the good will he had developed with the local tribes. Said one islander: "Claiborne was soe well beloved of the Indians that in case hee had had goodes sufficient to have trucked with them hee would have gott a greate deal more than hee did, and more than any other whatsoever in that country."

It was estimated that the cost to Claiborne for saving the trading post "amounted unto att least a thousand pounds sterling yearely." Claiborne himself declared: "I suffered mutch losse in my estate, under went many perills and dangers of life, indured hard voyages and many wants and tooke unspeakable paines."

But the worst was yet to come.

Three

Claims and Counterclaims
1632-1634

"Wee claim Right of Possession."

It was a claim that William Claiborne would repeat and never surrender in the lengthy war over his Chesapeake Bay settlements. In addition to Kent Island, his main base of operations in the upper Chesapeake, and Palmer's Island, situated at the mouth of the Susquehanna River, he also settled Popeley's Island (now Poplar), which he gave to his cousin Richard Thompson, and Claiborne's Island, which washed away. "These Claiborne settlements," wrote Eugene L. Meyer, "were the first by any English-speaking people in what would later become Maryland."

Priority was but one of Claiborne's arguments for his right to Kent and the other islands. Not only did he get there first, but he also purchased and occupied the property, then governed it under the authority of Virginia. Yet he faced a number of obstacles in the struggle to keep his real estate, the most important being the Calverts whose royal patent permitted them to set up a proprietary colony on lands that had belonged to Virginia under its original charter. But perhaps the enemy that ultimately defeated Claiborne's plan to center his trading empire in Chesapeake Bay was the vacillation of Charles I.

One problem with the reign of Charles I was his equivocation, his tendency to muddy the waters. He liked the idea of being king but did not want to be burdened with the king's responsibilities. His manner of governing was rarely to act but to react through a committee, a minister, or some commission. If members of the commission were lax in executing the royal instructions or if the minister sometimes interpreted those instructions to reflect his own proclivities, the king might not know about it, or even care. While this practice of simply endorsing the actions of his agents freed him from involvement in the routine of running the government, it also failed to keep him fully informed about issues and events that were critical to the welfare of both himself and his subjects—and it may explain why so often he was unable to make up his mind. Of course, the problem could have been compounded by the fact that he was extremely shy; he had an embarrassing stammer that limited him in dealing with his ministers and advisers.

Charles I believed that he was answerable to his God alone, that he owed his subjects no rationale for his action or lack of action. In May 1625 he defied the English church and ignored Parliament by marrying a Catholic, Henrietta Maria, the sister of the French king, Louis XIII. It must have been a comic affair. With Charles in England, the wedding took place in Paris at Notre Dame. There Henrietta Maria married Charles's proxy, the Duke of Chevreuse, who, because he was a Huguenot, was not permitted to enter the cathedral until after the nuptial mass. A month would pass before the new queen joined her husband (whom she had never seen). Charles was twenty-five; she was fifteen.

The history of Charles I shows that he assumed a role of such divine whim that his reign was one of continual contradiction. On the one hand he tried to impose the Episcopal Church of England on Presbyterian Scotland, on the other he extended encouragement to England's Catholics. The autocratic stand toward his native Scotland led to war; lenience to Catholics was probably a concession to his young queen, although he thought of himself as "a Catholic Christian" who rejected Rome's ritual trappings. He enforced harsh trade regulations on royalist Virginia, while taking a passive position toward the Puritan colonies in New England. Yet at home, where chaos was often the rule of the day, he opposed the Puritans who controlled Parliament through their dominance of the House of Commons. To Sir George Calvert, first Lord Baltimore, he granted territory taken from Virginia to create Maryland, then he staunchly defended those Virginians who opposed Baltimore's claim.

Calvert was far from defeated by his unsuccessful attempt in 1629 to create a colony on Virginia land. He tried and failed again in February 1632 when he asked for a large slice of Virginia south of the James River. Calvert then applied for rights to the Eastern Shore, arguing that a strong English colony in that area would check the encroachment of the Dutch. His application defined the request as "that whole peninsula laying between the ocean on the east and the great Bay of Chesapeack on the west and between Cape Charles on the south and Delaware Bay on the north." Though opposition from Virginians and friends of the old Virginia Company caused the request to be rejected, the Privy Council recommended that Calvert submit a new application placing the southern boundary at Watkins Point, near the Pocomoke River midway up the Eastern Shore, rather than Cape Charles (thereby excluding the Claiborne plantation at Accomac but including Kent and the other Claiborne islands in the upper bay). When the charter was issued on June 30, 1632, the boundaries were set from a point near present-day Philadelphia on the north (including portions of southern Pennsylvania) to the Potomac River on the south, winding westward to the river's source in the Allegheny Mountains, then eastward from the mouth of the Potomac across the Chesapeake to the Atlantic, and up Delaware Bay (including the present state of Delaware). Calvert and his heirs were created "true and absolute Lords, and Proprietaries of the Countrey," over which they would exercise royal power and privilege. To Charles I and his successors, they were obligated to deliver two Indian arrows "every yeere on the Tuesday in Easter weeke; and also the fifth part of all Gold and Silver Oare within the limitts aforesaid, which shall from time to time happen to be found." The new province was to be called Maryland (*Terra Maria*) in the honor of Charles's Catholic queen, Henrietta Maria.

George Calvert, son of a wealthy Yorkshire farmer of Flemish origin, was born about 1580. After earning his degree at Oxford University, he traveled extensively on the Continent before being promoted to the king's Privy Council by the powerful Robert Cecil, Earl of Salisbury, for whom he named his eldest son Cecilius. He was a highly refined man respected for his intelligence. Popular at court and a particular favorite of James I because of his support in Parliament of the king's royalist policies, Calvert was knighted in 1617 and appointed secretary of state, a post he held until his conversion to Catholicism in 1625. At that time, James I made him Baron of Baltimore in the county of Longford, Ireland.

From 1609 until 1620, Calvert was a member of the Virginia Company. He was a member of the Council for New England in 1622, and in 1625 a member of the Privy Council responsible for executing the king's order to annul the Virginia Company's charter. As early as 1620 (when William Claiborne was about to set out on his voyage to Virginia), Calvert purchased a tract of land on the southeastern peninsula of Newfoundland, between the Trinity and Placentia Bays. He later received a royal grant for all of Newfoundland, which he governed as a palatinate, giving him the absolute rule of a king. He named the palatinate after Avalon in Somerset County, England, which, according to ancient traditions, wrote Hale, was where the Holy Grail had been brought, "the birthplace of Christianity in Britain. Not the Christianity of Henry VIII, but the true faith as good Catholics interpreted it." Calvert's Avalon was to be as much a haven for England's persecuted Catholics as a base for lucrative trade with the Indians.

But it was not an auspicious undertaking for George Calvert. In 1627 he and his family were greeted at Newfoundland by a harsh climate and a rocky soil impossible to cultivate. Within two years he had to inform Charles I that hardships made it necessary to evacuate Avalon for a "climate in the New World where the winters were short and less rigorous." What he wanted was to remove himself and forty persons to Virginia, and enjoy the same prerogatives he had been granted for Avalon. In return, Calvert offered to "spend the remainder of his days enlarging the king's empire in that part of the world."

Charles I advised Calvert to return home but, before receiving the king's letter, he sailed with his family for Jamestown. There he received a cold reception and (as shown earlier) failed to acquire his patent when Virginians argued that, as a Roman Catholic, he was unable to swear to the king's supreme authority in the Protestant colony. Among the personal indignities suffered by Calvert was a tirade from assemblyman Thomas Tindall who threatened to knock him down. John Barth included the early Virginia episode in his novel, *The Sot-Weed Factor,* when Charles Calvert relates the arrival of his grandfather, the first Lord Baltimore, at Jamestown:

> *There he was met by Governor Pott and his Council (including the blackguard William Claiborne, archenemy of Maryland, who for very spleen and treachery hath no equal in the history of the New World), all of 'em hostile as salvages and bent on driving Grandfather away, for fear Charles would grant him the whole of Virginia...*

This apparent victory for Virginia did not discourage George Calvert. It simply meant that he would have to be more persuasive with the king's commissioners and his friends on the Privy Council.

In the meantime, Claiborne was joined on Kent Island by his half-brother and half-sister, the Reverend Richard and Gertrude James. Certified by the Bishop of London, Reverend James conducted Maryland's first service of the Church of England in the small fort at the southern end of the island. The Jameses were accompanied on their journey by Claiborne's brother Thomas, who became ill soon after his arrival on the island and died.

Another relative, Claiborne's cousin Richard Thompson, was appointed the island's chief assistant, responsible for hiring slaves from the James River plantations to help in the planting of tobacco and to handle menial services. Gradually, as signs of the disastrous fire disappeared, Kent Island took on the appearance of prosperity, of which the centerpiece was Crayford manor, located on the western side of the island. On the southeastern bank, Claiborne established a second plantation; he called it Romancoke, a Powhatan Indian word that he would reuse many years later to name his estate in New Kent County, Virginia.

In 1632 Claiborne was appointed a commissioner and commander of Accomac. That same year he was commissioned by the governor to investigate the Dutch activity in the north. His mission was to determine what could be done to block any southward movements similar to their recent settlements near the Hudson River and Delaware Bay. He also hoped to purchase a large stock of Dutch trading goods to supplement the short supply coming from his London partners, who answered his concerns with their own complaints about the venture's lack of profits. Though Claiborne was credited with being shrewd in the art of trading, he was a poor bookkeeper; he found it difficult to differentiate between company and personal transactions.

The Privy Council's solution to checking the Dutch seizure of English territory in America was to establish a colony that would squeeze the Dutch into as narrow an area as possible; hence, the 1632 charter that made Sir George Calvert proprietor of Maryland. But before the royal seal was be put on the charter, Calvert died.

All of the charter's rights and privileges were inherited by the son, Cecil (Cecilius) Calvert, who at age twenty-seven became the second Lord Baltimore. Like his father, Cecil had attended Oxford; unlike the father, he had never received a royal commission or displayed any interest in North America—until he acquired the Maryland charter, which he would pursue with "consummate prudence and tact," said Lyon G. Tyler. In 1623 he had married Anne Arundel, whose father had joined his brother-in-law the Earl of Southampton in 1605 in the first attempt at locating a sanctuary in America for England's Catholics. Anne Arundel County was named after his wife.

Cecil Calvert
Second Lord Baltimore
(1605-1675)

Cecil Calvert would not personally command Maryland. As its true lord and proprietor, he would own all the land, enjoy all revenues from it, control the appointment and dismissal of all officials, but he would rule the province from England—although his instructions to the colony dated November 13, 1633, said that "he hath deferred his owne coming till the next yeare, when he will not faile by the grace of god to be there." That he never went to Maryland was because he had to remain in England to protect his charter against constant attacks by the old Virginia Company.

Maryland's governor would be Lord Baltimore's twenty-year-old brother Leonard, who had participated in the Newfoundland venture and was better prepared to carry out the royal directive "to make warre, and to pursue the Enemies and Robbers ... as well by sea and by land, yea, even without the limits of the said Province, and (by Gods assistance) to vanquish and take them, and being taken, to put them to death by the Law of warre, or to save them at his pleasure, and to doe all and every other thing which unto the charge and office of a Captaine Generall of an Army belongeth."

Of course, the man Maryland was most likely "to make Warre" on was William Claiborne, who enlisted other Virginians in opposition to the territorial rights granted to Lord Baltimore—rights that would allow him to restrict Virginia's fur trade in Chesapeake Bay and in that region on the colony's northwestern frontier. It was a realistic concern: Lord Baltimore told Leonard Calvert to find a Chesapeake site that was convenient for trade with both the English and the Indians; and to encourage the Indian trade, he would send along such trading materials as beads, ivory, kettles, combs, axes, hoes, and Sheffield steel knives.

On July 3, 1633, in reply to the objections of Claiborne and his fellow Virginians, the king's commissioners said "that things standing as they doe, the Planters on either syde shall have free traffique and Commerce each with the other and that neither parte shall receive any fugitive persons belonging to the other, nor doe anie Act which may drawe a Warre from the natives upon either of them." Lord Baltimore would retain his patent and the two sides were expected to coexist in a spirit of cooperation "as becomes fellow subjects of the same state." Cooperation was the same as surrender to Claiborne, who urged the Virginia council to continue negotiations. On November 22, as Leonard Calvert was about to sail for America, another petition to the king's commissioners argued that the petitioners had been:

at a very great charge in transporting of men, cattell, discovering of trade, building of houses, and setling upon an island, by them named the Island of Kent within the greate Bay of Chessepiak in Virginia. Which being comprehended within the limitts of the Lord Baltimores Patent obteyned by his Lordshipp since the petitioners said great charge and setling there. They most humbly beseech your Honors that it may not bee taken from them but that they may have your Lordshipps order to enjoy the same with freedome of Trade without any interruption, and ... that the said Lord Baltimore may settle in some other place.

It was obvious the Virginia petition had been ignored when Leonard Calvert's two ships, the *Ark* and the *Dove*, sailed into the lower Chesapeake Bay on February 27, 1634. Worried about the reception he would receive at Point Comfort, Calvert had stopped in the West Indies to stock the *Ark* with enough provisions to last through the early months of setting up the new colony.

The *Dove* carried some two hundred passengers, separated into gentlemen adventurers and indentured servants or laborers, plus two commissioners and two Jesuits, Father Andrew White and Father John Altham. Though the colony was advertised as a refuge for England's oppressed Catholics, the majority of the recruits were Protestants and most of them were in the laboring class. The men of rank were mainly Catholics and they would receive the land grants in return for a yearly rent paid to Lord Baltimore. Since the passengers had to be sworn to an official oath of supremacy and allegiance to the king before the ships left England, the Catholics (who could not conscientiously take an oath which denied papal authority) were forced to conceal themselves. Extremely sensitive to the religious aspect of his American venture, Lord Baltimore had instructed his brother to

preserve unity and peace amongst all the passengers on Shipp-board and [to] suffer no scandall nor offence to be given to any of the Protestants, whereby any just complaint may heereafter be made, by them, in Virginea or in England, and [to] that end, they cause all Acts of Romane Catholique Religion to be done as privately as may be, and ... instruct all the Romane Catholiques to be silent upon all occasions of discourse concerning matters of Religion; and that the said Governour and Commissioners treate the Protestants with as much mildness and favour as Justice will permitt. And this to be observed at Land as well as at Sea.

From Point Comfort the Maryland ships sailed up the James to Jamestown where Calvert, resplendent in his cloak, white doeskin boots, and plumed hat which he flourished, presented Governor John Harvey a royal letter commanding the Virginians to provide food and assistance.

Harvey would later report to England: "I sent unto them some Cowes of myne owne, and will do my best to procure more, or any thinge else they stand in need of." The gesture did not please the other Virginians who, according to one report, "would rather knock their Cattell on the heades than sell them to Maryland." One of the Marylanders wrote that Virginia's council desired "noethinge more than our ruine."

It was impossible for Claiborne to conceal his animosity, and Leonard Calvert responded in kind. Claiborne was told that because Kent Island was located within the boundaries of the Maryland patent, he could remain there only as a tenant of Lord Baltimore, and that he would have to obtain a Maryland license to trade. This mandate was contrary to Lord Baltimore's instructions. Calvert had been warned to avoid confrontation and to send Claiborne a letter as soon as it was convenient. The purpose of the letter was to try to placate Claiborne...

to invite him kindly to come unto them, and to signify that they have some business of importance to speake with him about from his Lordshipp which concernes his good very much; And if he come unto them then that they use him courteously and well, and tell him that his Lordshipp understanding that he hath settled a plantacion there within the precincts of his Lordshipps Pattent, wished them to lett him know that his Lordshipp is willing to give him all the encouragement he cann to proceede; And that his Lordshipp hath had some propositions made unto him by certaine merchants in London who pretend to be partners with him in that plantacion [and] that they desired to have a grant from his Lordshipp of that Iland where he is: But his Lordshipp understanding from some others that there was some difference in partnershipp between him and them [and] that they made somewhat slight of Captain Clayborne's interest, doubted lest he might prejudice him by making them any grant his Lordshipp being ignorant of the true state of their business and of the thing they desired, as likewise being well assured that by Captain Clayborne his care and industry besides his charges, that plantacion was first begunn and so farr advanced, was for these reasons unwilling to condescend unto their desires, and therefore deferred all treaty with them till his Lordshipp could

*truly understand from him how matters stand between them, and
what he would desire of his Lordshipp...*

Calvert was also instructed to assure Claiborne that Baltimore
intended "not to do him any wrong, but to shew him all the love and
favour that he cann," confident that Claiborne, like a good subject to
the king, would conform to the Maryland patent. Should Claiborne
refuse, Calvert was to "lett him alone for the first yeare," during which
time he would learn what he could about Claiborne's plans and
strength. At the year's end, Claiborne's behavior would determine
further directions from Lord Baltimore.

Had Leonard Calvert followed instructions, the relationship
between Claiborne and Baltimore might have been less hostile, and
Claiborne might have lived a respected man of rank and property in
both Virginia and Maryland. As it turned out, Claiborne lost no time in
appealing to fellow members of the Virginia council for advice and
support in solving his Kent Island problem. On March 14, 1634, just
thirteen days before the settlement of Maryland, the council upheld
Claiborne's appeal: An attack on Claiborne was an attack on Virginia,
which had as much right to Kent Island as to the land on which
Jamestown stood—since both were clearly within the territorial rights
originally assigned to the colony.

The two main objections raised by Maryland authorities to the
Claiborne title to Kent Island were: Virginia had no right to the land in
question because the charter of the Virginia Company had been
revoked in 1624 when Virginia became a crown colony, thereby
leaving unsettled regions subject to distribution at the pleasure of the
king; and even if Virginia did retain jurisdiction over the disputed land,
Claiborne had no official land grant from Virginia and therefore his
settlement was merely a trading post.

Virginians countered that the colony's legal rights to lands within
the boundaries established in the Virginia Company charters had been
repeatedly confirmed by royal proclamation. James I had declared that
while the repeal of the Virginia Company's charter had nullified the
company's sovereignty, it did not infringe upon the colony's territorial
rights. This was restated in a letter from the Privy Council to the
Virginia government on July 22, 1634:

> *We do hereby authorize you to dispose of such proportions of lands
> to all those planters being freemen, as you had power to do before
> the year 1625.*

Claiborne's royal license authorized him and his associates to trade and traffic "in all seas coasts rivers creekes harbours lands and territories in neere or about these partes of America for which there is not allready a patent graunted to others for their sole trade." The license was issued in May 1631, more than a year before the Maryland charter was handed to the first Lord Baltimore.

Both sides could find strong arguments in the language of the Maryland charter:

For Baltimore—The charter mentioned specifically "all Ilands and Iletts within the Limitts aforesaid." And it granted Baltimore the "Jurisdictions, Privileges, Prerogatives, Royalties, Liberties, Immunities, and Royal rights, and Franchises of what kind soever temporall, as well by Sea, as by land, within the Countrey."

For Claiborne—The charter granted Baltimore the right "to transport an ample Colonie of the English Nation unto a certaine Countrey hereafter described, in the parts of America, not yet cultivated and planted, though in some parts thereof inhabited by certaine barbarous people, having no knowledge of Almighty God ..." Not only was William Claiborne's island *cultivated and planted* but it also was occupied by at least one hundred English Christians duly represented in the Virginia assembly.

No matter how sound the argument for Claiborne's side, Lord Baltimore knew the right people: he had the power of the royal establishment behind him. Of course, William Claiborne had courage and tenacity. In refusing to accept Baltimore's authority over him, or his island, or his trading venture, he declared "that if my Lord's plantacion should surprize or take any of his boates, he would be revenged though he joined with the Indians in a canoe." He would continue to trade in the Chesapeake as freely as before.

Yet, despite the arguments and threats, the Maryland charter was clear in its intent that Baltimore's province should "not from henceforth bee held or reputed as a member, or a part of the land of Virginia..."

John Marshall later observed that Lord Baltimore's settlement of Maryland was "the first example of the dismemberment of a colony, and the creation of another within its own original limits, by the mere act of the crown."

It was to be an act of war.

Four

Taunts and Threats
1634

Henry Fleet, Claiborne's chief rival in Chesapeake fur trade, offered his services to Leonard Calvert as a guide and interpreter. Having maintained an active trade with the Piscataways and other tribes living along the Potomac and its tributaries, he knew the country well and was ideally suited to help the Marylanders find a proper site for their first settlement. On March 25, 1634, Fleet directed the expedition up Chesapeake Bay to a small island which the Marylanders christened St. Clement's. There they erected a cross and took possession "In the name of the Savior of the World and of the King of England." Then they celebrated the first Roman Catholic mass in English America, conducted by Father Andrew White.

In the *Dove* and a pinnace which Calvert had purchased at Point Comfort, some two hundred Maryland settlers sailed up the Potomac to survey the lands controlled by the Piscataway Indians. Fleet suggested the area was too high in the river and led the expedition back to a point near the bay where the Potomac connected with a small tributary. The location impressed Calvert because it formed "two excellent bayes, wherein might harbour three hundred saile with great safetie." At the nearby village, the Yoacomacoes were persuaded by Fleet to give up a plot of their land to Calvert, in exchange for farming implements, cloth, and hatchets. The plot was situated on a bluff overlooking the tributary and included a few crude huts and cultivated fields. A witness to the transaction was Father White, who wrote that "the Governour took possession of the place, and named the Towne Saint Maries." Ignatius Loyola, founder of the Jesuits, was proclaimed the colony's patron saint.

Father White asked: "Is not this miraculous that a nation ... should like lambes yeeld themselves [and be] glad of our company, gieving us houses, land, and liveings for a trifle?" It was not as miraculous as it seemed. The Yoacomacoes, constantly terrorized by the Susquehannocks, had hoped to find sanctuary across the Potomac River in Virginia; they were more than eager to take the English valuables for a plot of land they planned to abandon.

St. Mary's City became Maryland's first capital, and Calvert called it "as noble a seate as could be wished." From the time it was founded on March 27, 1634, St. Mary's would flourish. In fields already cleared and cultivated by the Indians, they immediately planted tobacco; and by year's end, the corn crop was sufficient to trade with the New Englanders for saltfish and other provisions. Thus Henry Fleet's influence on Calvert's decision to choose the Yoacomaco site removed many of the hardships that had confronted Virginia and the New England colonies. Asked by the grateful Marylanders to remain in St. Mary's, Fleet was given a two-thousand-acre plantation, elected to the Maryland assembly, and offered an opportunity to share in the Maryland beaver trade. This news must have distressed William Claiborne, who had learned in his early encounters with Leonard Calvert that fur trading in the upper Chesapeake was restricted to traders who recognized Lord Baltimore's authority over that region, and that each of the licensed traders was required to pay a tenth of the value of the furs he got from the Indians as "a Custome to his Lordshipp." He also would learn that violators and their vessels would be confiscated and that the fur traffic he had begun to develop to the north would be stopped.

It was clear from the outset that Lord Baltimore's Maryland palatinate was first a profit center, and then a refuge for maltreated Catholics and disgruntled Protestants. And he knew that the profits would depend largely upon his ability to attract settlers in large numbers. High on his list of recruiting appeals were the "rewards of station and preferment, which will be liberally given in honor of worth, valor, fortitude and noble needs." But the most important inducement was the promise of land, based on the same headright system that had been successful in Virginia. Land was granted to all those who, at their own expense, transported others (usually indentured servants) to the colony: one hundred acres was given for each able-bodied man and fifty acres for each woman or child. And, according to Father White, "two thousand acres of good land" would be allotted to anyone who "shall pay a hundred pounds to carry over five men; whether they shall think best to join us themselves, or entrust the men and money to those who shall have charge of this matter, or to anyone else, to take care of them and receive their share of the lands." Indentured servants could be anyone from prisoners of war and convicted felons to respectable young men and women who hoped to better themselves in America but could not afford to pay for the voyage; by signing a contract, or indenture, they agreed to provide a stipulated period of servitude (usually four years) in return for the passage and upkeep. As explained by Samuel Eliot Morison, the headright system created profits not by selling land but through annual rents paid to Lord Baltimore; it also supplied the labor and was the principal means of populating the colony.

Financial gain was perhaps secondary to Father White. In his *Account of the Colonie of the Lord Baron of Baltamore*, he said "the place abounds not alone with profit, but also with pleasures." He was enthralled with Maryland's natural attributes: "The climate is serene and mild, not oppressively hot like that of Florida ... nor bitterly cold like that of New England; but preserves, so to speak, a middle temperature between the two, and enjoys the advantages, and escapes the evils of each." On the east the province "is washed by the ocean; on the west it borders upon an almost boundless continent, which extends to the Chinese Sea. It has two very large arms of the sea [the Chesapeake and Delaware Bays], both of them abounding in fish. There are various notable rivers. The chief of these they call the Attawomech [Potomac], a navigable river running eastward 140 miles, where there is such lucrative trade with the Indians that a certain merchant in the last year exported beaver skins to the value of 40,000 gold crowns." Father White described the wide variety of seafood, the swine and deer in such numbers "they are rather an annoyance than an advantage," the vast herds of cows and wild oxen "fit for beasts of burden and good to eat," the many trees, vines, and fruits, the ravenous eagle and the "birds of prey which live, for the most part, on fishes, and partridges no larger than quails, but in almost endless numbers." He noted "the soil so rich, as to afford three harvests a year." His litany of Maryland's wonders seemed to have no end, and included the "hope of finding gold" and the expectation "that the provident industry and long experience of men will discover many other advantages and sources of wealth."

A pamphlet entitled *A Relation of Maryland*, published to instruct those persons planning to emigrate to the new colony, said the Marylanders were fortunate in settling among "the Piscataways, a gentle and peaceful tribe of Indians who received them with hospitality and gladly furnished them with shelter and provisions." In addition, "they procured from Virginia Hogges, Poultrey, and some Cowes, and some male cattell, which hath given them a foundation for breed and increase, [and] have already increased in Maryland to a great stocke, sufficient to serve the Colonie very plentifully." They also had "a Water-mill for the grinding of Corne." Thus, in St. Mary's, "within the space of sixe moneths, was laid the foundation of the Colonie of Maryland."

The pamphlet discussed the trade provisions:

> *If hee bee minded to furnish himself with Cattell in Virginia, his best way is to carry a superfluitie of woolen, or linnen cloth, callicoes, sayes, hatts, shooes, stockings, and all sorts of clothing; of Wine, Sugar, prunes, Raisins, Currance, Honey, Spice, and Grocery wares, with which hee may procure himself cattell there, according to the stocke hee dealeth withall. About 4 or 5 Pound laid out here in commodities, will there buy a Cow: and betweene 20 and 30 shillings, a breeding Sow. The like Commodities will furnish him either there, or in Maryland, with Hogges, Poultry, and Corne. Hee may doe well also to carry a superfluitie of Knives, Combes, and Bracelets to trade with the women natives; and some Hatchets, Howes, and Axes to trade with the men for Venison, fish, Turkies, Corne, Fawnes ...*

The pamphlet also described the region of the Chesapeake that would be of most interest to Maryland's prospective settlers:

> *The ordinary entrance by Sea into this Countrey is betweene two Capes, which are distant each from the other about 7 or 8 leagues, the South ... is called Cape Henry, the North, Cape Charles. When you come within the Capes, you enter into a faire Bay, which is navigable for at least 200 miles, and is called Chesopeack Bay, and runneth Northerly: Into this Bay fall many goodly navigable Rivers, the chiefe whereof is Patomack, where the Collony is now seated ... navigable for 140 miles [and] begins to bee fresh about 2 leagues above Patomack Towne. The next River Northward is Patuxent, which at the entrance is distant from the other about 20 miles, and is a very pleasant and commodious River; Its fit for habitation, and easie to bee defended, by reason of the Ilands, and other places of advantage, that may command it; from thence, untill you come to the head of the Bay, there are noe more Rivers that are inhabited: There dwell the Sasquehanocks, upon a River [the Susquehanna] that is not navigable for our Boates, by reason of Sholes and Rockes; but they passe it in Canoos; At the entrance thereof, there is an Iland which will command that River. Uppon the East side of this Bay lie very many Ilands which are not inhabited, where are store of Deere.*
>
> *On the Easterne shoare of the Countrey, which lieth upon the maine Ocean, are sundry small Creekes, and one likely to proove a*

very commodious harbour, called Matsoponque [Machepongo Inlet,
Northampton County, Virginia]; neere the mouth whereof, lieth an
Island of about 20 miles in length, and thence about 6 leagues more
Northerly, another Iland called Chingoto [Chincoteague], and
about seaven leagues beyond that, to the North, opens another very
large faire Bay, called Delaware Bay ... about 8 leagues wide at the
entrance, and into it, there falls a very faire navigable River.

This Countrey is generally plaine and even, and yet hath some
pritty small hills and risings; Its full of Rivers and Creekes ...
Springs and small Brookes: The Woods for the most part are free
from underwood, soe that many may travell on horsebacke, almost
anywhere, or hunt for his recreation.

It was not very long before Henry Fleet lost interest in the Maryland
fur trading enterprise, and his popularity declined. Some settlers even
accused him of trying to incite the nearby Patuxent Indians who suddenly had grown suspicious and distrustful of them. Fleet attempted to
shift the blame by spreading the rumor that William Claiborne had told
the Patuxents that the recent arrivals at St. Mary's were *Waspaines*, or
Spaniards, who had come to kill all the Indians. It was easy for Marylanders to believe the worst of the Kent Island trader, especially when
Thomas Cornwallis, one of Calvert's commissioners, backed up Fleet's
claim that he had actually stopped the Patuxents from joining Claiborne
in an attack on St. Mary's. When the rumor was relayed to Governor
Harvey, he ordered that Claiborne be placed in custody in Jamestown
until the charges could be investigated by a joint commission of Virginians and Marylanders.

The commission met with the accused at the Patuxent Indian village
on June 20, 1634, with the Maryland delegation headed by the governor's younger brother, George Calvert, and the Virginians by Claiborne's friend, Samuel Matthews. Based on the record of proceedings
in the Maryland Archives, when the chief of the Patuxents was asked
why he believed the newcomers at Yoacomaco (St. Mary's) to be
Spaniards, he revealed it was a misunderstanding. The Patuxents had
been unable to differentiate between *Waspaines* and the hated *papists*,
two terms picked up from the gossip they heard from Fleet and other
traders, all of whom were spirited Protestants. Moreover, they were
confused by the hostility between the newcomers and the English with
whom they were already acquainted, having been told that the Spaniards were traditional enemies of the English. When the Patuxent chief
was asked specifically whether Claiborne had referred to the Marylanders as Spaniards, as reported by Fleet, he said, "Noe ... Captaine

Clayborne did never speak any thing to him of them." This was confirmed by the chief of the Piscataways. Then the Patuxent chief wondered why the white men "should take notice what Captain Fleete said ... he doth lye soe much."

The commissioners signed a document which vindicated William Claiborne and promised that "when they came to speak with Captaine Fleete, all the lyes would redound uppon him and lye uppon him as high as his necke, and at last breake his necke." Though Governor Calvert apologized, he was as determined as ever to rid Maryland of Claiborne—who would find on his return to Kent Island that Baltimore's agents had "shott att" the islanders in order to disrupt their trading activities. They also had already evicted the freemen who, with Claiborne's permission, had settled Popeley's Island.

The Virginia Council sent a letter of complaint to the lords of trades and plantations, whose reply supported the Virginians under the rights laid out in the Virginia Company charter. This of course was ignored by the man who had helped dissolve the company. In September 1634 Lord Baltimore instructed his brother to arrest Claiborne, if he continued to trade in Maryland waters without a license, and seize Kent Island. Virginians said this was contrary to the order of July 1633 in which the king's commissioners had encouraged the parties "on either syde [to] have free traffique and Commerce each with the other," and in London Charles I came to the defense of Claiborne and his partners in the following declaration:

> *By a petition exhibited unto us by our lovinge subjects William Cloberry, John Dela-Barre and David Moorehead, wee are given to understand that whereas by our Comission they had formerly traded, planted and inhabited an Iland neare to Virginia which they have nominated the Kentish Iland, and have to their greate charge not only sent over a good number of people and Cattell but bought the Interest of the Natives in that Iland. Nevertheless (as they informe) by pretence of a later pattent granted to Lord Baltimore, some of his Companies have assaulted them and hurt some of the said Inhabitants, and endeavor to drive them out and prohibbit their trade; which is contrary to justice and the true intention of our grant to the said Lord: wee doe therefore heereby declare our expresse pleasure to bee that the said planters be in noe sore interrupted in their trade or plantation by him or by any other in his right: But rather that they bee encouraged to proceed cheerefully in soe good a Worke.*

The king's document concluded:

> *And wee prohibitt as well the Lord Baltimore, as all other pretenders under him or otherwise to plantations in those parts to doe them any violence, or to disturbe or hinder them in their honest proceedings and trade there.*

It was signed at Hampton Court on October 10, 1634.

Confident of their rights, the Kent Islanders expanded their trading activity in the upper Chesapeake, now with an eye on the Indians living on the Patuxent River near St. Mary's. This bold contempt for the Maryland charter did not go uncontested. In total disregard of the king's directive, Lord Baltimore got his well-connected friends in England to pressure the governor of Virginia to come to his support; whereupon the king's secretary asked Harvey to continue his assistance to the Maryland government "against the malicious practices of William Clayborne," and even persuaded the inconsistent Charles I to do the same (except there was no mention of Claiborne or "malicious practices" in the king's letter).

As his governor was offering new expressions of friendship and assistance to his enemy, Claiborne was forced to spend most of his time at Kent Island strengthening both his land and water defenses against possible attack by the Marylanders. To this end, he had his boatyard build a large pinnace, the *Long Tayle*, which was armed and placed under the command of Captain Thomas Smith, with a twenty-man crew. The Kent Island fleet also included a new shallop, the *Start*; a sloop, the *Cockatrice*; a small pinnace, the *Firefly*; and other armed vessels. At the same time, Claiborne was busily expanding his operation by clearing more land, erecting new buildings, recruiting more islanders, importing more "trucking goods invoiced by William Cloberry at twelve hundred pounds," although Claiborne estimated the goods were "worth not half the charge." He also was trying to keep the peace with the Wicomesse and Susquehannocks who finally realized they were being swindled by some of the local traders. In December 1634 he wrote: "This yeare, wee were much hindered and molested by the Indians falling out with us and killing our men and by the Marylanders hindring our trade."

A letter written by Captain Thomas Yong, while commanding a fleet of vessels trading with Virginia, provides a picturesque summary of the Claiborne-Baltimore controversy as it unfolded in 1634. The following excerpt describes the initial encounter between Yong, at anchor aboard his vice-admiral, and Claiborne's barque, a small trading vessel propelled by sail or oar:

As soon as wee were now come to an anchor we descried a small barke coming out from Point Comfort, which bare with us, and about half an hower after she came to an Anchor cloase aboard our vice admirall. Wee thought she had bene some vessel bound from Virginia to New England, whither the Inhabitants of Virginia drive a great trade for Indian Corne. I sent my Leiutenant aboard her to enquire whence she was and whither she was bound, and withall to learn what he could both concerning the State of Virginia and Maryland, which is my Lord Baltimores Collony, as likewise on what termes those two Collonyes were, and what correspondence they had one with another and with the Indians also. [Yong's lieutenant] found this Barke to bee a vessel of Virginia belonging to one Captayne Cleyborne, who liveth upon an island within my Lord of Baltimores Territory called the Ile of Kent. [After] salutations ... they fell in talke concerning my Lord of Baltimores Company, who arrived heere in March last. Hee discovered that there was growne great discontents between my Lords company and him which hee seemed to excuse as well as hee could though even by some words that now and then fell from him unawares my Leiutenant saith a man might read much malice in his heart towards them. After some two houres, my Leiutenant brought Captayne Cleyborne with him aboard my ship where hee remayned till the morning.

Yong refers to an attempt by Virginia and Maryland officials to meet with Claiborne to resolve the differences between him and Lord Baltimore, a meeting which Claiborne did not attend:

[From Claiborne] I understand that the Governour of Virginia, Sir John Harvie, had bene in Maryland at the plantation there which is called St Maries, there to have heard and composed the differents which were growne between those of my Lords Collony and this Cleyburnes; [and] in his company were Captayne Calvert Governour of Maryland, Captayne Cornwallis, Mr Hawley, and other principall gentlemen of Maryland, and that they were come thither purposely for the composing of those differents, but that [Claiborne] for his part purposed not to bee there, but to retire himself to his own Plantation, under pretence that hee went thither to take order for the securing thereof against certayne Indians, who had lately as hee understood killed a man and a Boy of his, but I playnly perceaved that the principall and mayne reason for his retreat was to absent himself from that meeting.

Any bias shown by the letter writer is reflective perhaps of Yong's friendship with the Calverts:

*I found the man subtle and fayre spoken but extreamely averse
from the prosperity of that Plantation. Hee alleaged that my Lords
company had accused him to the Governour of Virginia for
animating, practizing and conspiring with the Indians to supplant
and cutt them off: that the Governour had appointed certayne
commissioners of this Collony to joyne with certayne other
Commissioners of my Lords Collony to examine the truth of that
accusation and that uppon their information hee purposed to
proceed herein according to Justice. That accordingly they had
examined the matter and had found noe grounds for those
accusations and soe hee conceaved that the purpose of their
comming was now only to make a reconciliation, but that for his
part hee purposed not to bee there. On the other side, hee pretended
that heertofore hee had borne very good correspondence with them
and that hee had furnished them with hoggs and other provisions
and done them what curtesies were in his power, till my Lords
people had given directions for the taking and surprizing his boates,
that went to trade, and likewise of his owne person. After which
discourse hee parted from me, telling me, though I perceaved
afterwards hee ment it not, hee would meet me at Point Comfort, but
hee came noe more to me.*

*The next morning I weighed as soon as the tide served and about
eleven of the clocke I came to an anchor within Point Comfort,
where now I ride. Heere I understood that the Governour was hard
by, and as soone as I had fitted my dress I tooke boate with intention
to have awaited uppon the Governour on shoare, but ... I descried
his Barge on the River making towards our shipp ... but perceaving
me row towards him [he] stood towards my vice admirall, whither
also I stood and gott into the ship before him, who as soone as hee
perceaved me aboard presently entered therein. After I had saluted
him hee was pleased to treat me with much curtesy and great
affection; to whome I presented his Majesties commands, which I
have also found him most effectually and affectionately observe, on
all occasions, wherein I had cause to require his assistance.*

Yong's letter relates the Thomas Cornwallis version of Claiborne's
alleged endeavor to incite the Indians against the Marylanders:

*After some time I took Captayne Cornewallis aside and told him
what discourse had passed between Cleyborne and me. Hee
answered me that this Cleyborne had dealt very unworthyly and
falsely ... That he had also labored to procure the Indians to
supplant [the Marylanders] by informing them that they were
Spaniards [who] had a purpose to destroy them and take their*

Countrey ... That the Indians had ... bene dissuaded by one Captayne Fleete who had in former times lived amongst them, and is now in good creditt with them. That Cleyborne had contrived divers other malitious plotts and conspiracies against them. That some others also of the principall Councellors of Virginia might justly be suspected to have animated Cleyborne to his foul practises. That his conspiracy and practices was proved against Cleyborne, both by the confession of the Indians and likewise by the confession of Christians taken upon oath. That hee himself publickly protested that if my Lords plantation should surprize or take any of his boates, hee would be revenged though hee joined with the Indians in a canoe. That heerupon the Governour of Maryland complayned thereof to Sir John Harvie, the Governour of Virginia, who forthwith tooke the matter into his consideration. Upon hearing the accusation of the one and the defence of the other, it was ordered that Cleyborne should remayne confined in the hands of Captayne Matthews and Captayne Utie, two councellors of State in Virginia, though both of them private friends to Cleyborne ... and that the two should forthwith, taking Clayborne along with them, repaire to my Lords Plantation in Maryland, where also two Commissioners, namely Captayne Cornewallis and Mr Hawley, chosen for that Collony, should bee joined with them, and that they should take on both sides interpreters and from thence goe in company together to the Indians and examine the truth of this examination, but that Cleyborne was not to bee present at the examination. And that they should make a true relation of the state of the business to the two Governours who would expect them in this plantation, at Maryland. But precisely and expressly ordering them that they should bee carefull in noe case to suffer any conference to bee had with the Indians, on either side, either directly or indirectly.

But these two Captaynes, taking along with them Cleyborne, went towards Maryland, not with any purpose (as it afterwards appeared by the sequelle) to comply with the Governours order of Virginia, having subtlely and sinisterly inveigled into their company two very young gentlemen of my Lords collony (whereof the one was a younger Brother of my Lord [George Calvert], *the other of Sir John Winters), with faire words, finding them in a joviall humor, perswaded them to accompany them to the examination of these Indians, and so taking these for my Lord Commissioners, instead of going to my Lords plantation at Maryland or giving any notice of their arrivall in those parts, they take this advantage and, with these young gentlemen which themselves tooke and chose in place of Commissioners, they goe directly to the Indians, taking with them also Cleyborne and a servant of his for their Interpreter, and there, in the presence of Cleyborne, examine the Indians uppon such Articles and with such Interrogatories as they thought would best suit with their purpose. When they had done they putt this examination in writing, and after they had themselves signed it, they procured also these two young gentlemen to put their hands also thereunto as taken before them.*

This examination they sent to my Lords plantation at Maryland by one of the Councell of Virginia ... and in his company came also one of the Indian Kings called the King of Pattuxunt, procured by them ... to justifie the truth and impartiality of their proceedings, Laboring by their indirect proceeding to cleerr Cleerborne from his crimes and ... to incense and exasperate the Indians both against my Lords people and against those other Christians also who had informed them thereof, suggesting and intimating to them that my Lords were turbulent people, who cared not what false pretense and suggestions they framed to deprive others of their estate, which it was evident they labored to wring out of the hands both of Indians and Christians also, that soe in Fine they might become Lords of that Countrey ...

Concerning his complaynt that my Lords company would have surprized his boates and him, Captayne Cornewallis told me that Cleyborne had been offered all faire correspondence, with as free liberty to trade as themselves, but hee refused it, wherefore the Governour gave order to forbid him to trade. That concerning the surprizall of his person (though his carriage towards them very well desserved it) yet it was only a meere supposition and jealousy of his owne, without any grounds.

Yong warns that the Claiborne situation could become so dangerous as to warrant intervention from England:

This, so farre as I can learne, is the true state wherein my Lord of Baltimores plantation stands with those of Virginia, which perhaps may prove dangerous ... if there bee not some present order taken in England for suppressing the insolence of Cleeborne and force his [compliance] and for disjoynting this faction, which is soe fast linked and united as I am perswaded will not by the Governour bee easily dissevered or over ruled without some strong and powerful addition to his present authority by some new power from England, and it will bee to little purpose for my Lord to proceed in his collony against which they have soe exasperated and incensed all the English Collony of Virginia as heere it is accounted a crime almost

*as heynous as treason to favor, nay allmost to speak well of that
Collony of my Lords.*

Yong writes favorably of the Virginia governor distrusted and hated
by most Virginians:

> *The Governour only of Virginia (a gentleman in good faith in my
> judgment of a noble mynde and worthy heart) out of his care to
> observe his Majesties commands signified to him by his Royall
> letters and also out of his own inclinations hath carried himself very
> worthily and respectively towards them and is ready on all occasions
> to give them all the assistance and furtherance that possibly hee can,
> though thereby hee had acquired to himself extreame hatred and
> mailice from all the rest of the countrey.*

Captain Yong wrote of his visit to Jamestown, at the invitation of
the Virginia governor, and of "the strength and power of some factious
and turbulent spiritts" of the governor's council, "for heere in this place
all things are carried by the most voyces of the Councell, and they are
for the most part united in a kind of faction against the Governor." He
named Claiborne's ally Samuel Matthews as "the head and cheefe sup-
porte" of that faction:

> *This gentleman, as I am told ... hath bene the incendiary of all
> this wicked plott of Cleybornes and yet continues to bee the
> supporter and upholder of him, and except my Lord finde some
> meanes speedily and in a very exemplar maner to curb and
> suppresse this mans insolencies, hee will dayly find more and more
> practizes and treacherous conspiracies contrived against him ...*
>
> *Nor is that other instrument of his of whome I spake before,
> namely Cleyborne, less carefully to bee lookt unto, since his
> practizes, though they bee not soe publick as the other insolencies,
> yet are they not lesse dangerous to that Collony, yea and to the
> security of the peace of this very land and government of Virginia,
> where I have bene informed that some of the Councellors have been
> bold enough in a presumptuous manner to say, to such as told them
> that perhaps their disobedience might cause them to bee sent for into
> England, that if the King could have them hee must come himself
> and fetch them.*

If Matthews was the "incendiary" on the Virginia side of the Claiborne-Baltimore quarrel, then his Maryland counterpart was the hot-
headed commissioner, Cornwallis, aided and abetted by Captain Fleet.
As to whether it was Fleet or Claiborne who had created suspicions
among the Patuxents toward the Marylanders, it probably depends

upon whose account to accept; the historians appear to be about equally divided. It is, of course, hard to believe that the Virginia commissioners were able to "sinisterly inveigle" George Calvert, the younger brother of Lord Baltimore, into engaging in some conspiracy to support Claiborne; although he did ultimately move (or was driven) from Maryland to Virginia.

Before the year ended, Governor Harvey inaugurated a move in England to have William Claiborne removed from his office as the Virginia secretary of state, on the grounds that he was lax in his administrative responsibilities, that in spending so much time at Kent Island he seldom put in an appearance at Jamestown—although the real reason for dismissing Claiborne was his opposition to the Maryland charter and the governor's hope that this support of Lord Baltimore would gain his assistance in recovering a large sum of money due to Harvey from the royal treasury. Claiborne was replaced by Richard Kempe, one of Baltimore's close friends.

The Virginians threatened to retaliate.

But Claiborne was temporarily distracted by a problem closer to home. Joan Butler, wife of the man who would soon become his brother-in-law, was accused of using profane language to blemish the character of her neighbor, Marie Drew. She was tried in the Accomac court which Claiborne had been instrumental in establishing in 1632. When found guilty, Joan was sentenced to ducking (dragged over King's Creek at the stern of a boat) unless she retracted her crude behavior in church. She chose the ducking.

Following the incident, her husband Thomas Butler apparently took leave of his post at Kent Island and sailed to England, alone.

Five

"*Pyracie and Murther*"
1635-1638

In the spring of 1635, Elizabeth Butler and her brother John arrived in Virginia. Almost immediately, the twenty-four-year-old Elizabeth and thirty-four-year-old William Claiborne were married in a formal ceremony performed by the Reverend Richard James at the Jamestown church. The couple spent a brief honeymoon at Claiborne's Kecoughtan plantation in Elizabeth City, which was now one of the eight counties or shires created in Virginia. From there the couple sailed up the Chesapeake to Kent Island where they christened the recently completed Crayford manor. For the islanders it was a time of celebration, blighted only by the foreboding that Claiborne and the Marylanders were rapidly moving toward open warfare.

For months the Kent Islanders had been conducting a highly profitable fur trade with the Susquehannock Indians. Then one day a Maryland trader named Cyprian Thorowgood "sett saile from the mouth of the Patuxent in a small pinnace manned with seven men." His objective was to investigate the trading opportunities in the upper Chesapeake when his vessel reached Palmer's Island at the mouth of the Susquehanna River. There he observed that a Claiborne boat had obtained hundreds of skins in trade with the Indians. "As soon as they see us coming," wrote Thorowgood, "Claiborne's men persuaded the Indians to take part with them against us, if we did offer to take their boat. But the Indians refused, saying the English had never harmed them, [and] neither would they fight soe neare home." Whereupon the Claiborne men "weighed their anchour" and sailed away—leaving the field open to Thorowgood, who said that "what skins the Indians had left, they brought to us, and went home to fetch what more they had ... which made in all two hundred and thirty." On hearing the tale, Claiborne placed Captain Thomas Smith, one of his most trusted aides, in charge of an armed company responsible for strengthening his hold on Palmer's Island.

Thus, a short time later, Sergeant Robert Vaughan of Maryland was unaware of the dangers awaiting him and his crew when their small trading pinnace approached the island. Even before they had stepped ashore, Captain Smith ordered his armed men to seize their boat and its "great quantitie of trucking commodities." Informed by Smith that they had invaded Claiborne's trading territory, Vaughan and his crew were taken to Kent Island as prisoners. Claiborne kept the "trucking commodities" but released the prisoners and their pinnace, with a warning to the officials at St. Mary's that he would continue to resist invasions by Maryland into his rightful domain. Response from the Maryland assembly was to pass an act "censuring Smith for Pyracie."

This only aggravated Claiborne's contempt for Lord Baltimore. On April 5, 1635, he dispatched Captain Smith, now in command of the new pinnace *Long Tayle*, to trade for much-needed corn at an Indian village on the south side of the Patuxent, just a few miles from St. Mary's. Smith and his islanders were confronted by an armed company headed by a Captain Humber and Henry Fleet, who questioned their right to be trading in Maryland without authorization. Smith said their rights were protected "by vertue of his Majesties Commission and letter graunted to Captain Claiborne," a copy of which he presented to Fleet. The Marylanders scoffed at the document as "a false coppie and grounded uppon false informacion" and reminded Smith that Claiborne was not licensed to trade within the province. When Fleet and his men boarded the *Long Tayle*, Smith demanded to see the commission "by which they tooke us, but they would shew mee none." Unarmed, he could only watch as Fleet put ashore some of the crew who were forced "to travell to St. Mary's on foote," defenseless against any hostile Indians they might encounter. Smith and the remainder were ordered "to weigh Anchor and fall Downe towards" the Maryland capital city. The *Long Tayle* was confiscated on the order of the governor to take "all vessels which they should find trading within the Province of the Lord Baltimore." Smith, in his account, concluded the episode:

Seeing noe hopes of having our vessell againe, I desired the Governor wee might returne home, [which he granted] but said hee was sorrie hee had noe boate to send us home in, although having at that tyme three boates riding at his dore. I told him if there was noe other way I would make some meanes by the Indians, which hee graunted I should doe. The next day wee were sent away in a cannow

without either peece or victuals but one peece which I had myselfe,
haveing twenty leagers to goe without any meanes but such as wee
should find from the Indians. With great danger it pleased God to
send us home.

From that moment on, both sides of the territorial dispute took the
precaution of arming their vessels.

Before Smith reached Kent Island, Claiborne had news of the incident at the Patuxent and he considered it a breech of the king's directive
which entitled him to trade anywhere in the Chesapeake Bay region.
Immediately he sent Lieutenant Radcliffe Warren in "a wherry with
some men to demande the pinnace that the Marylanders had taken."
Unable to find Claiborne's pinnace in the Patuxent, Warren did capture
"a boate with some trucking stuffe belonging to Mariland" and brought
it back to Kent Island.

When Smith arrived to report the loss of the *Long Tayle*, he also announced that Calvert had dispatched a large pinnace on a trading voyage to the Eastern Shore. Lieutenant Warren saw this as a chance to
surprise the Marylanders and seize a boat the equal of the *Long Tayle*.
On April 23, aboard the sloop *Cockatrice*, Warren and a crew of thirteen men arrived at the Eastern Shore and sailed up the Pocomoke
River. Soon they sighted the *St. Helen*, one of Maryland's largest pinnaces, near a Pocomoke Indian village where Claiborne's islanders had
been trading for several years. Warren devised a hasty plan by which he
and his men would quietly slip up on the Maryland vessel, quickly
board it and capture the crew. But at that moment he spotted the *St.
Margaret*, an even larger and more menacing pinnace coming from a
nearby cove.

In what some have exaggerated as "the first naval engagement in the
New World," the *Cockatrice* approached the two pinnaces with Warren
and his men, waving "gunnes and pistols, swords and other weapons,"
threatening to charge the Marylanders in hand-to-hand combat.
Suddenly, the flash of gunfire, the locking of swords, and the cries of
anger and anguish echoed from the swamps and woodlands bordering
the Pocomoke. The battle was brief. Under the command of Thomas
Cornwallis, the victorious Marylanders suffered but one casualty. For
the outmanned Virginians, the combat was costly in the lives of
Lieutenant Warren and two members of his crew; the ten survivors,
most of them wounded, returned to Kent Island aboard the *Cockatrice*.
Cornwallis was hailed a hero by Baltimore and awarded four thousand
acres on the Patuxent, described at the time as a "very pleasant and

commodious River ... fit for habitation, and is easie to bee defended, by reason of the Ilands and other places of advantage."

Members of the Maryland general assembly addressed the attack on Cornwallis, declaring that "Ratcliffe Warren, John Bellson and William Dawson [Claiborne men killed in the action] did discharge their gunnes against the said Thomas Cornwaleys and his company." The three were denounced "as felons pyrates and murthers."

It was suggested later that the story related to Captain Smith about the trading voyage to the Pocomoke River was contrived by Cornwallis in order to lead Claiborne and his islanders into a trap. True or not, the Pocomoke engagement was an aggressive act by Virginians as well as Marylanders; and once the news of the event circulated, great passions excited both colonies.

In the eyes of Maryland authorities Claiborne was not to be trusted; not only was he a pirate but also a man who would steal corn from the Indians and sell it for tobacco. Of course, members of Virginia's council championed William Claiborne in his struggle to protect the colony's territorial rights, and many had expressed bitterness over Maryland's earlier attack on the *Long Tayle*. One of the councillors was the fire-brand Samuel Matthews, who accused the Marylanders of taking "Captain Claiborne's pinnaces and men, with the goods in them, whereof they had made a prize and shared the goods amongst them, which action of theirs Sir John Harvey upheld contrary to his Majesty's express commands."

Understandably, Virginians considered their governor a man of many sins. "In the contests between Cleyborne and the proprietary of Maryland," wrote Charles Campbell, "Harvey sided with Baltimore, and proved himself altogether a fit instrument of the administration then tyrannizing in England. He was extortionate, proud, unjust, and arbitrary; he issued proclamations in derogation of the legislative powers of the assembly; assessed, levied, held, and disbursed the colonial revenue, without check or responsibility; transplanted into Virginia exotic English statutes; multiplied penalties and exactions, and appropriated fines to his own use." Just recently he had suppressed a petition addressed to Charles I by the general assembly complaining about the crown's monopoly of the tobacco trade; then when the Virginians protested, Harvey had the ringleaders arrested on the grounds of treason.

Charges of treason also were leveled at Harvey; and on April 28 the governor was removed from office by the Virginia council. The council then elected as acting governor John West (a son of the first governor of Virginia) and then summoned the general assembly, which ratified the council actions. With threats that "hee would be pistolled or Shott" if he returned, Harvey was shipped to England in the care of two council members who went along to present their complaints to the king. The ship carried a letter to Sir John Coke, secretary of state, from William Claiborne at Elizabeth City. The letter discussed the "tumults and broyles, wrongs and oppressions perpetuated with an high hand and not without undue courses in the alteration of Government and such violence acted as hath shewed itself in the effusion of native bloud." Claiborne said that he was "sett uppon [by] cruell neighbours" who not only trampled his rights but also showed themselves to be "such enemies or such men to deale with as would spurne at the Kings Royall Commands uppon them." He concluded: "Wee beseech a speedy signification of his Majesties pleasure to abate the fury of our adversaries."

Now that Harvey was gone, the Virginians felt secure in the leadership of John West, who wrote to the Lords Commissioners for Plantations: "Without infringing his Majesties grant to the Lord Baltimore wee have taken the nearest course for avoyding of further unnaturall broyles between them of Maryland, and those of the Ile of Kent, as also Captain Clayborne the Commander of the Ile of Kent towards those of Maryland."

West was unaware that Claiborne, determined to be revenged for the humiliating defeat at the Pocomoke and the earlier loss of the *Long Tayle*, was embarking on another of the "unnaturall broyles."

First, he gave the following instructions to Philip Taylor, a young Accomac trader who had helped him settle Kent Island:

> ... the Marylanders have taken my Pinnyce the Long Tayle, with her Company and some other of my men tradeing in other places. Now whereas his Majesties Commission to myselfe warranteth mee in trade with the natives, and for as much allsoe his Majesties gratious Letters in America doe declare his expresse pleasure to be against this their violent and exorbitant proceedings, and contrary to justice and the true intent of his Majesties grant to ye Lord Baltomore, These are to desire you, that you would with the first opportunity, with such Company as are appoynted for you, sett sayle to Patawomack and Patuxant Rivers, or elsewhere, and to demand of them my said Pinnyce and men: and if you can obtaine them, to take possession of them for my use and bring them agayne unto this place, Or missing of them, make stay of such boates of theirs as you can light on. Wherein I beseech you proceede without Violence unless yt

bee in lawfull necessary defense of yoreselfe, especially to avoyd any bloodshed or makeing any assault uppon any of them, and to this end I require all yor Company to bee obedyent and assistant unto you as yf I were there myselfe.

Claiborne then ordered Captain Thomas Smith to take command of the *Cockatrice* and proceed to the Eastern Shore where Cornwallis, aboard the *St. Margaret*, had been seen trading with the Indians on Great Wicomico Bay (now Pocomoke Sound). Smith succeeded in seizing the Cornwallis pinnace along with its furs, corn, and other trading goods—which would be condemned by Maryland authorities as an act of "felonie and pyracie."

The scenario was different, however, on the Potomac where, according to Taylor's report, the "Marielanders did severall tymes vyolently with armed men gonnes and Indyans assault [his] Pynnace and boate and tooke ... the said Pynnace with all the goods therein." He said he managed to escape by convincing his captors that he was on a friendly mission intent only on trading for corn to save the Kent Islanders from starvation; but Hale wrote that Taylor's escape may have been contrived, following a truce arranged by the Virginia and Maryland governments after Claiborne's arrival in Jamestown with news of the bloody encounter. Two Virginia commissioners had been dispatched to St. Mary's to demand that the Marylanders "desist their violent proceedings." Calvert, concerned about retaliations against his own people, agreed to the truce.

The return of captured boats and cessation of attacks by both sides led to a period of peace that left Claiborne in possession of his islands and free to trade without having to bow to the authority of Lord Baltimore. With all quiet on the upper bay, Claiborne bought another pinnace and equipped it to increase his Kent Island trading activity. The boat was named *Elizabeth* after his wife who, a few months later, gave birth to a son, William Claiborne Jr.

Records also show that the newly formed counties in Virginia were to be governed like the English shires, with a sheriff at the top and a lieutenant responsible for the county's military. The man named as lieutenant of Accomack County was Claiborne, who was still one of the county's prominent landowners; his deputy was Obedience Robins. Since it was also necessary for Claiborne to oversee his supply depot and milling operations in Elizabeth City, as well as keep in touch with his powerful friends in Jamestown, he obviously spent a great many hours sailing back and forth from his trading post and manor house on

Kent Island. Of course, how long he would enjoy the freedom of sailing the Chesapeake would depend upon the king's commissioners, who were expected to clarify the territorial contradictions between Virginia and Maryland.

When Harvey arrived in England, an angry Charles I arrested his two Virginia escorts and accused the Virginia council of preempting the royal authority. On complaint of Lord Baltimore, he instructed John West, Samuel Matthews, George Menefie, and other councillors considered Maryland's most outspoken foes to appear in England to answer for their belligerence. In the meantime, Harvey would remain as a guest of the king until the commissioners decided the status of Kent Island and other Claiborne properties located within the boundaries defined in the Maryland charter.

There could be only one decision as far as Baltimore was concerned. While insisting that he remain the absolute lord proprietor of Maryland, he was so bold as to apply for the office vacated by Harvey and now held by acting governor West; in short, that he be appointed the royal governor of Virginia. In appealing to the king, he promised that his administration of Virginia would increase the royal revenues by some eight thousand pounds yearly "without laying any new, or other tax or imposition on the Planters, than what they now do, and will most willingly pay."

Had such a plan been agreed to, it would have promoted an active rebellion in Virginia and more than a one-man war against Maryland. The king ignored Lord Baltimore's application, and to reinforce his own control of Virginians and rebuke the dangerous precedent they set by deposing a royal governor, Charles I ordered Harvey back to the colony to resume his former office.

In early 1636 William Cloberry's suspicions that Claiborne was mishandling company funds led him to request his Virginia partner to come to England to render an accounting of his trade activities. Claiborne's inclination was to ignore the request. From his viewpoint, Cloberry should answer to him. His London partners had not shipped any supplies to Kent Island since December 1634, and during that time he had been using his own private income to maintain the trading operation. Consequently, Claiborne had confused his assets with those of the company and suggested that Cloberry "send a yonge man over" to sort out the joint stock accounts. It proved to be an unwise suggestion.

The "yonge man" arrived in December 1636 with a letter urging Claiborne to comply with Cloberry's request for a company meeting in

London. The letter also introduced George Evelin, a new partner (having purchased the one-sixth share of John Delabarr) who would assume responsibility for managing the Kent Island plantation and trading activity while Claiborne was away. Claiborne was surprised and annoyed that the company would make such a decision without his consent; he would have preferred to turn over the management to his brother-in-law John Butler. Still, Evelin was a partner and seemed to be loyal to the best interests of the Kent Island enterprise; he had reaffirmed the company's trading rights, insisting that William Claiborne's commission from Charles I "was firme and strong against ye Maryland Pattent," and vilified Leonard Calvert as "a very Dunce and blockhead when hee went to schoole." So Claiborne felt it would be useful to go to London where he could smooth over any disagreements with Cloberry and, at the same time, press for his rightful claim to the properties appropriated by Lord Baltimore. But he was cautious enough to ask Evelin for "a Bond of three thousand pounds sterling" as assurance that he "would not sell, or make away, the Plantacion or Iland, or anie parte thereof, unto the Marielanders, or anie others, and not to remove or carry away anie of the Servaunts from the Iland." Claiborne said the bond must be delivered before he could hand over the trading post and its goods to Evelin; whereupon Evelin replied that Cloberry's power of attorney was all he needed to take command of the plantation.

In February 1637 a large supply of trading goods arrived from England, consigned to Evelin at Kent Island. The ships that brought the supplies also brought another group of indentured servants and Sir John Harvey who, as the restored governor, would organize a new council and resume his tyranny of Virginia for two more years.

Thus, in May, after making arrangements for the management of his Virginia holdings, Claiborne and his family boarded the pinnace *Thomas* for the voyage to England. As the vessel sailed through the Virginia capes, Claiborne must have been concerned about the return of a Virginia governor in sympathy with Lord Baltimore, the fate of his Chesapeake Bay trading enterprise now that George Evelin was in control of Kent Island, and the appointment of Evelin's brother as one of Harvey's councillors; such worries had led him to fortify his island in the Susquehanna as a possible retreat should Maryland forces invade Kent Island or in case the king and his commissioners ruled against him.

Semmes wrote that Evelin "was as zealous as Claiborne had been in resisting the claims of the Maryland authorities to Kent Island" during the early months of his administration. But this enthusiasm completely changed after Claiborne's departure. Friendly overtures from Governor Calvert to visit St. Mary's seemed to convince Evelin that "the Marylanders had the better title to the island." Soon he neglected the interests of both Claiborne and Cloberry and opened negotiations in which he was commissioned commander of Kent Island.

When the Kent Island inhabitants, including "about one hundred and twentie men able to beare armes," were assembled and told that the island had been surrendered to the Maryland authorities without a struggle, they were astonished. When Evelin tried to turn them against Claiborne, in the hope of winning their support, they were enraged at the betrayal of this man who had sworn earlier "that the Marylanders had nothinge to doe with the Isle of Kent." When John Butler asked him "whether he was an Agent for Cloberry & Company or for the Marylanders," Evelin declared he was the agent for both. Later he wrote that after "hee had seene the Governor of Marylands Pattent" he realized "that hee was formerly mistaken & wondred that Cloberry & Company should be soe mistaken ... but hee himselfe now understood it better." He tried to persuade the islanders that "it would be better to live under the Government of Maryland than under the Government of Virginia, for my Lord Baltimore hath ye Pattent & the Island was his." He wrongly described Claiborne's commission as one which "was for Nova Scotia and other places near New England & did not give Authority to trade in the Bay of Virginia, or Maryland," and then promised the islanders that they would be free to "carry their Commodities & their Tobacco & pipestaves into what Country they would" if they recognized Baltimore's authority. The Kent Island inhabitants, under the joint leadership of John Butler and Captain Thomas Smith, refused to betray Claiborne or to accept the command of Evelin, whom they blamed for the dramatic decline in trade with the Indians and the resultant threat of starvation.

In response to these "insolencies" against his appointed commander, Governor Calvert authorized Evelin "to attach the persons of John Butler and Thomas Smith, of the Ile of Kent, and them to keepe in safe custodie without baile or mainprise [surety]; and to have them before me at St Maries with all convenient speed there to answere the severall crimes of sedition, pyracie and murther, which shall be on the Lord Proprietors behalfe objected against them." Butler and Smith, under the protection of the islanders, were able to avoid arrest, even when

Calvert told the islanders that they could choose one of their own as "theire commander."

In June 1637 Evelin obtained a warrant from Harvey to seize all the boats, servants, and supplies in Virginia that belonged to Cloberry & Company as well as those held by William Claiborne, on the grounds that he was in debt to the company. He also asked the Virginia governor to place Butler under bond not to "meddle with anye thinge" related to the company. At the time, Butler was at Jamestown defending Claiborne's right to Palmer's Island before the governor's council. It was to Butler's good fortune that Calvert's opposition was represented by Jerome Hawley, a Maryland trader who happened to be in sympathy with Claiborne—so much so that Hawley ultimately moved to Virginia where he was appointed treasurer and councillor.

In November, under pressure from Evelin to use military force to gain control of Kent Island, Governor Calvert wrote: "I gathered togeather about twenty musketteers out of the Colony of St. Maries and appointing the command of them to Captain Cornwallis whome I tooke as my assistant with me, I sat saile from St. Maries towards Kent about the latter end of November, intending to apprehend Smith and Butler if I could, and by the example of theire punishment to reduce the rest to obedience." The expedition, hindered by winter weather, was delayed two months.

In February 1638 Calvert learned that St. Mary's was in danger of attack by the Susquehannock Indians. He informed Lord Baltimore that the Susquehannocks had accused the Marylanders of supporting an enemy tribe "against them two yeares before (which we never did though they will needs thinck so) and that they were incouraged much against us by Thomas Smith who had transplanted himselfe with other English from the Ile of Kent the last summer to an Ileand at the head of the bay fower miles below the falls called Palmers Island and understanding likewise that they had planted and fortified themselves there by directions from Captain Cleybourne with intent to live there independent of you (because they suppose it out of the limits of your Province)." The Maryland council, concerned that the Indians would be given "gunns to our further harme," concluded that Maryland "could more easily make peace with these savages" if Claiborne's men were removed from Palmer's Island. This was the governor's signal to act.

With Claiborne in London haggling over company accounts with Cloberry, Calvert and a force of thirty Marylanders set sail for another attempt at securing Kent Island, accompanied by Cornwallis and

Evelin. This time the weather was calm and just before sunrise, they landed "without notice" at Long Point, on the southern end of the island where Claiborne's house was located "within a small fort of Pallysadoes." The islanders were caught by surprise and the fort was taken with no resistance, which pleased Calvert who said he had hoped to land without "giving untymely notice unto Butler and Smith of my comeing."

The governor set up headquarters at Crayford and rounded up all the islanders in the area and had them quartered in the fort. Next, he dispatched ten of his musketeers to Butler at his nearby plantation, The Great Thicket, to acquaint him with the situation "and command his present repaire unto me." Claiborne's brother-in-law was brought to Crayford and placed under arrest.

Calvert then ordered his sergeant, Robert Vaughan, to take six musketeers and capture Thomas Smith at his Beaver Creek home which was located across the creek from Butler's plantation. Smith, not knowing that Butler had been captured, was easily taken.

The triumphant Calvert, in writing to Lord Baltimore, said that he charged "both the chiefe delinquents ... with theire crimes and afterward committed them Prisoners aboard the Pinnass [with] a gard over them." Butler and Smith were "delivered into the custody of the sheriffe at St. Maries."

Pardons were offered to all other Kent Island inhabitants who were willing to submit to the Maryland government, and those who accepted the offer were given title to the land they occupied. The "fur factory" (as the trading post was often called), Claiborne's plantation at Crayford, and all of his personal possessions were attached. Evelin was placed in command of the island and instructed by Calvert to see that new boundaries were surveyed and laid out. The governor then returned to St. Mary's where he ordered "a grand inquest" to determine Captain Smith's crimes against the province. But Calvert decided to show clemency toward Butler, hoping that if he won his support the other islanders would follow.

Smith was tried without the advice of counsel. According to the Acts of Assembly for March 14, 1638, Smith "was called to the barre being indicted of pyracie." It was "demanded that the prisoner might be brought to triall upon his indictment." After all but one member of the assembly found Smith to be guilty, the assembly president, Cornwallis, pronounced the sentence:

Thomas Smith you have been indicted of felonie and pyracie; to your indictment you have pleaded not guilty, and you have been tried by the freemen of this generall Assembly, who have found you guilty, and pronounce this sentence uppon you, that you shalbe carried from hence to the place from whence you came, and thence to the place of exeqution, and shalbe there hanged by the neck till you be dead; and that all your lands, goods & chattells shalbe forfeited to the Lord Proprietarie, saving that your wife shall have her dower; and so God have mercy uppon your soule.

Again Calvert showed leniency, issued a stay of execution, and released the prisoner on bail. The reprieve was short-lived. Smith, on his return to Kent Island, remained steadfast in his loyalty to Claiborne and instigated a rebellion against Maryland authorities. Calvert invaded the island with a force of fifty musketeers, easily put down the insurrection, and captured Smith. This time the court tried him not as a pirate but confiscated all of his "lands, goods & chattels" and hanged him as a rebel.

About Butler, the governor wrote to Lord Baltimore: "I have taken him out of the sherrifs custody into my owne howse, where I intend to have him remayne, until I have made further experience of his dispositions, and if I can win him to a good inclination to your Service." Then, after asking the Maryland assembly to censure Butler for acts of piracy, he decided to put him in charge of Kent Island's militia—an ironical appointment that would make William Claiborne's brother-in-law responsible for suppression of mutiny and civil disorder. He thought it would appease the islanders who were inflamed over the execution of Captain Smith. But before the appointment was announced, the Kent Island inhabitants revolted. Calvert acted quickly to make certain that the island was "wholly reduced" by rounding up all cattle, supplies, and servants (those belonging to inhabitants as well as to the Cloberry company) and transporting them to St. Mary's, then hanging some of the islanders "without any tryall of Law." Nothing was spared: Palmer's Island was renamed Fort Conquest and abandoned as a trading post, ending the "great trade of beaver and other furrs" which Claiborne had envisioned with "the mountayn Indians" living near the "lakes of the river of Canada."

The Maryland assembly then passed *An Act for Trade with the Indians,* which "did by publique proclamation prohibite all persons whatsoever from tradeing with any Indians of this Province without leave or lycense from or under his said Lordshipp."

The assembly also passed *An Act for the Government of the Ile of Kent*, which read in part:

> Be it Enacted By the Lord Proprietarie of this Province of and with the advice and approbation of the same that the Iland commonly called the Ile of Kent shall be erected into a hundred & shall be within the County of St Maries (untill another County shall be erected of the Eastern shoare and no longer) and shall be called by the name of Kent hundred and the Commander of the said Iland from time to time appointed by the Lord Proprietarie or his Leiutenant Generall ...

George Evelin, the one man whom Calvert singled out for praise in the capture of Kent Island, soon lost interest in the island and turned over his estate (Claiborne's manor house at Crayford) to his younger brother and went home to England. He was succeeded as commander by Robert Philpot who, because of his inability to govern, was replaced by William Brainthwaite, a Calvert kinsman, who then was succeeded by Giles Brent who turned to John Butler for advice.

When Butler died in 1642, he left his Maryland estate not to his sister Elizabeth, living in nearby Virginia with her husband William Claiborne, but to his brother Thomas who had returned to England in 1634. Thomas Butler sold the estate to a John Abbott.

In February 1638 Claiborne had been declared an outlaw in Maryland. After the capture of Kent Island, the Maryland assembly passed *A Bill of Attainder* against him, charging that he was

> notoriously knowen to have committed sondry contempts, insolences and seditious acts against the dignity, government and domination of the Lord Proprietarie of this Province, and to have conspired and contrived sondry mischievous machinations and practices with the Indians of these parts to the subversion and destruction of this colony and the people thereof; and to have used and exequted sondry Magistracticall and regall powers and jurisdictions, within this province and uppon the Inhabitants of the same, by levying of souldiers, appointing Leutenants and other Officers, imprisoning and otherwise punishing of Offenders, and by granting letters of reprisalls and Commissions for the exeqution of justice uppon the vessells and goods of the Leutenant generall of this Province, and of the people inhabiting this colony of St Maries, without any authority or Commission for exercising the same from our Soveraigne Lord the King, or from the Lord Proprietarie of this Province, or from any other Prince or State whatsoever ...

The assembly noted that "the said William Cleyborne had not onely continued his said insolences, mutinies and contempts against the Lord Proprietarie and the Government of this place but hath instigated and commanded sondry persons to commit the greivous crimes of pyracie and murther" during the April 1635 assault by the *Cockatrice* on the two Maryland pinnaces allegedly trading in the Pocomoke River. But since Claiborne could not be tried for his crimes because he had "fled and withdrawn himself out of the Province," the assembly demanded again "that he forfeit to the Lord Proprietarie all his lands and tenements which he was seized of on the said three and twentieth day of April in the year 1635. And that he forfeite to the said Lord Proprietarie all his goods and chattells which he hath within this Province at this present."

Meanwhile, in England, Lord Baltimore and Claiborne were competing for the favor of Charles I, who had referred the controversy to the Commissioners of Foreign Plantations, which had the power to amend or revoke charters and patents and make other laws governing the English colonies. Because Baltimore was represented by powerful interests, it was perhaps no surprise when the commissioners ruled:

> The Right & Tytle to the Ile of Kent & other places in question to be absolutely belonging to the Lord Baltimore, & that noe Plantation or Trade with the Indians ought to be within the precincts of this Pattent without Lycence from him.

The commissioners determined that Claiborne's claim was based only on "a Lycence under the Signett of Scotland" while Lord Baltimore's charter carried "the broad seal of England." Concerning Claiborne, the commissioners declared that

> noe Graunt from his Majestie should passe to the said Cleyborne or any others of the said Ile of kent, or any other parts or places within the said Pattent Whereof his Majesties Attorney & soliciter generall are hereby prayed to take notice. And concerning the violences & wrongs by the said Cleyborne & the rest complayned of in the said Petition to his Majestie their Lordshipps did now allso declare, that they fownd noe cause att all to relieve them, but doe leave both sides to the ordinary course of Justice.

Charles I muddied the waters again. In response to Claiborne's request for assistance, and unaware of the commissioners' decision, the king commanded Baltimore to permit Claiborne and his Cloberry partners to remain at Kent Island "and be safe in their persons and goods

... without disturbance or farther trouble by you ... till that cause be decided."

For Claiborne, it continued to be a losing cause. In Virginia, Harvey issued a proclamation on October 4, 1638, recognizing the validity of the commissioners' decision and prohibiting Virginians from trading in Maryland without Lord Baltimore's authorization. He lost again when his Maryland attorney George Scovell failed to recover his confiscated property after being told the Maryland courts were closed to Claiborne. Later, however, when examined by the High Court of Admiralty on the piracy charges brought against him by the Maryland assembly, Claiborne convinced the court of his innocence.

Of course, the redoubtable William Claiborne would continue to challenge the charter of Lord Baltimore.

Six

Cavaliers and Roundheads
1639-1643

When Governor Harvey and his Virginia council proclaimed Lord Baltimore's victory, William Claiborne was in London. Having lost Kent Island and other possessions in the upper Chesapeake, and perhaps his holdings in lower Virginia, Claiborne also faced in 1639 a suit filed by Cloberry & Company in the High Court of Admiralty. Of more than twenty allegations, the major charges brought against him were mismanagement, appropriation of money and goods belonging to the company, setting fire to the storehouses on Kent Island, and his refusal to give a proper account of goods bartered and received in trade with the Indians. He was even charged with conspiring with Lord Baltimore in a scheme that would deliver to Maryland the property and goods owned by the company.

Though Claiborne was in England at the time of the Kent Island fire, he was accused of leaving instructions to destroy the storehouses and their contents in order to make it impossible to arrive at an accurate account of the company's trading activity. Cloberry neglected to show how Claiborne would profit from the alleged arson since he was uninsured and also suffered loss.

Cloberry was accused of failing to transport supplies to Kent Island for the past five years, during which time Claiborne "did yearly send unto the said Cloberry and Companie severall quantities of beaver," which the company sold and had "not given Claiborne any part or account thereof, whereas the greatest part of the said beaver ... were bought with the proceeds of the said Claiborne's own estate ... and that the said Claiborne was allwaies more out of purse than all the rest of the said partners."

Moreover, said Claiborne, in order to maintain the company's interests, he had gone into personal debt, suffered other miseries, and, when captured by the Indians, was "like to be slayed by them and hath lost the use of his right arm."

Claiborne declared that his duties at Kent Island often made it necessary to ignore his responsibilities as "Secretary of State and Councell and Surveyor Generall." As a result, he "lost his said offices beinge worth at least 1000 pounds Sterling per annum."

Claiborne scoffed at the absurdity that he conspired with Lord Baltimore and accused Cloberry of duplicity in attempting to strike a separate deal with Baltimore that would exclude Claiborne, as was reported to him by the Maryland governor.

George Evelin's appointment as Cloberry's new representative at Kent Island was not only "contrary to their covenant and agreement," said Claiborne, but led to rebellion among the islanders and caused the trading enterprise to "come to ruine."

To clarify any mismanagement or confusion of company accounts, Claiborne attempted to explain the difficulties in trading with Indians:

> *Our trade with the Indians is always with danger of our lives; and that we usually trade in a shallop or small pinnace, being six or seven English men encompassed with two or three hundred Indians. And that it is as much as we can do to defend ourselves by standing on our guard with our arms ready and our guns presented in our hands. Two or three of the men must look to the truck that the Indians do not steal it, and a great deal of the truck is often stolen by the Indians though we look never so well to it; also a great part of the truck is given away to the Kings and great men for presents; and commonly one third part of the same is spent for victuals, and upon other occasions. And that the usual manner of that trade is to show our truck, which the Indians will be very long and tedious in viewing, and do tumble it and toss it and mingle it a hundred times over so that it is impossible to keep the several parcels asunder. And if any traders will not suffer the Indians so to do they will be distasted with the said traders and fall out with them and refuse to have any trade. And that therefore it is not convenient or possible to keep an account in that trade for every axe, knife, or string of beads or for every yard of cloth, especially because the Indians trade not by any certain measure as by our English weights and measures. And therefore every particular cannot be written down by itself distinctly. Wherefore all traders find it that it is impossible to keep any other perfect account than at the end of the voyage to see what is sold and what is gained and what is left.*

Claiborne would stand by his claim that "there was much due him from the said Cloberry and Companie for disbursements made by him for the said plantacion as he could make justly appeare by his accountes," but he was content to let an impartial arbitrator settle their differences. Of course, now that Maryland authorities had seized Kent Island and all property, goods, and servants belonging to Claiborne and Cloberry, any conclusion reached by the arbitrator was of no consequence. Claiborne would return to Virginia hoping to salvage at least his plantations at Elizabeth City and Accomac, and the tract on the Pamunkey River.

Meantime, Maryland's claim to Kent Island received official sanction from the general assembly. On February 12, 1639, the island's freemen were instructed "to chuse from amongst themselves two or more discreet honest men to be their deputies or Burgesses during the next assembly."

The following response from the islanders was read before the Maryland assembly on February 25:

> *Know all men by these presents both present and to Come that we the freemen of the Ile of Kent whose names are hereunder written have elected and chosen our Loving Friend Nickolas Brown Planter to be our Burgess or deputy during the next Generall Assembly at Saint Marys summoned to Begin on the 25th of February next [and] in Our names to assent to all and only such things as our Burgess shall think fit thereby Giving as free and full Consent unto all Laws and matters whatsoever written the said Assembly shall be agreed and Concluded of as if we our selves in person had Consented thereunto.*

The choice of Nickolas Brown as one of the island's representatives was endorsed by twenty-four freemen. The designation of a second Kent Island burgess, Christopher Thomas, was signed by a different group of twenty-five freemen, including one Thomas Butler (or Boteler) who may have been the Claiborne relative whose wife Joan had been sentenced to a ducking in King's Creek in 1634.

Before leaving England, Claiborne renewed earlier associations with Puritanism, the reform movement in the Church of England which had reached beyond theology to influence, and ultimately regulate, the political and social conduct in both England and America. Its dogma must have seemed to be more rigid than when he first embraced the movement at Cambridge. In his youth, he had been attracted to a fraternity of liberal thinkers whose religious reforms evolved into bold ideas of individual freedom and political equality; concepts that fostered the Country Party and its opposition to the Court Party, committed to the divinity of kings. Now, twenty years later, the Puritan movement— though it still called for limited monarchy and a stronger parliament— was controlled by the conservative element who, as guardians of English morality, were intolerant of anyone who differed with their views. That kind of morality was beyond the grasp of Claiborne who thought of himself as an independent Church of England man with Puritan tendencies that were planted in his early mercantile surroundings and cultivated during his university days.

But there was more to Puritanism than religion or politics; there was commercialism: the desire of the middle-class Puritan merchants to expand markets and increase revenues through colonization. Members of the Country Party suggested that Claiborne might recover his Maryland losses through the Providence Island Company, which was promoting Puritan settlements in the Caribbean. As described by Hale, the area "was boiling with Dutch, Danes, Frenchmen and Englishmen, all trying to invade the colonial dominions of Spain." And though the venture involved piracy and privateering, the Puritans considered these to be "legitimate methods of taking vengeance on the country which had despoiled half the world in the name of religion."

Claiborne's interest in the venture was influenced by Captain Nathaniel Butler, his wife's uncle, who had been named governor of Providence Island, an English possession. Butler was being financed by the company to equip an expedition for the purpose of fortifying the island and enlarging English presence in the Caribbean. To this end, Claiborne was offered the opportunity to purchase a grant to Roatan Island (three times the size of Kent Island) off the coast of Honduras; but he had to refuse the offer because he was short of funds: Claiborne had been unable to get a settlement from Cloberry & Company and Harvey had made it impossible to raise capital on his Virginia properties. There was nothing to do but go to Virginia and try to put his financial affairs in order.

Claiborne's arrival in Virginia was the signal for Harvey's exit. Pressured by George Sandys, Southampton, and other members of the old Virginia Company, Charles I named Sir Francis Wyatt the new governor. Wyatt, a member of the Country Party and the last of the company governors, was certainly no royal favorite. He was chosen only to silence the king's enemies in England and those frustrated Virginians whose grievances against the former governor had led to threats of violence. Wyatt reinstated the councillors replaced by Harvey, upheld Claiborne's claim to Kent Island, and then restored his Virginia holdings.

Claiborne also obtained a grant of three thousand acres on the south side of the river separating Maryland and Virginia; there he established a "Potomack" community for those followers who had been driven from Kent Island in 1638. Then, as his finances improved, he readied the home in Elizabeth City for his family, now including a two-year-old daughter, Jane, who was born in England and named after her maternal grandmother.

In 1640 the American colonies were not overly concerned about the civil strife heating up in England between the Puritan majority in Parliament and the royalist supporters of Charles I. But in time two of those colonies, Virginia and Maryland, would feel the heat of that conflict. The persistency of the old adventurers to revive the Virginia Company had won the parliamentary support and again a Virginia patent was issued to the company. This was but one of many affronts to Charles I in his dispute with Parliament, and he acted quickly to strengthen his hold on the crown colony by naming Sir William Berkeley, a true royalist, to succeed Wyatt. In early 1642, soon after the new governor reached Virginia, he urged the assembly to adopt a petition protesting the restoration of the company. That the petition was adopted over stiff opposition demonstrated the fidelity that Virginians would show to Charles I up to his tragic end. Of course, the action of the assembly was academic since the king had said that he would not consent to the introduction of any company over the colony.

Like his father, Charles I ruled England by the ancient and arrogant principle that the king was divinely endowed and could do no wrong. This arbitrary rule, indifferent to the concerns of the commoners, aroused resentment throughout England and was reflected in growing animosity toward the king in Parliament. But Charles I had never taken his opposition seriously. Earlier, he had reminded the House of Commons "that Parliaments are altogether in my power for their calling, sitting and dissolution: therefore as I find the fruits of them good or evil they are to continue or not to be."

As English king, Charles I was head of the Anglican Church. Though many of his enemies accused him of being a closet Catholic, he claimed to be a moderate Anglican who resented Puritan dominance of the House of Commons and condemned the excesses of his native Scotland's Presbyterianism. It was his attempt to force the English church on the Presbyterian Scots that erupted in a costly war that could not be supported by a treasury depleted by mismanagement and royal indulgence. Thus in 1640, after ruling without a parliament for eleven years, Charles I had not a sudden change of heart but a calculated change of policy. Already entangled in costly disputes on the Continent, the desperate need for money forced him to seek Parliament's approval to advance his plans for Scotland. But that support was withheld until the king agreed to limits on royal power with a corresponding increase in parliamentary participation in the government.

Among Parliament's charges against Charles I were his threats against members for speaking freely, support of the Star Chamber and other royal courts eroding the liberties of his subjects, condoning the abusive power of Anglican bishops and the cruelty of his ministers, and weakening the government to the point that England was not only at war with the Scots and threatened by invasions from Ireland but also distrustful of its flimsy peace with Spain.

The hated Star Chamber was abolished, the king was forbidden to collect money without parliamentary consent, and several of the king's chief ministers were executed. Parliament demanded to choose all future advisers, have complete control over the militia, and assist the crown in resolving religious differences. Finally, the king was obligated to summon future parliaments every three years.

Declaring that royal prerogatives were not negotiable, the king responded by arresting Parliament's leading members who were charged with attempting to deprive Charles I of his powers, of exaggerating the rights of Parliament, of inciting the English people to treason, and of plotting a war against the crown. When the king was accused of violating the privileges of Parliament, he in effect dismantled the traditional form of government on January 10, 1641, and left London. As a result, it has been argued that Charles I was a stubborn and incompetent king who failed in both his foreign and domestic policies and "voluntarily surrendered his sovereignty to Parliament." He would not return to London until nine years later as a prisoner.

In the meantime, England was at war with itself.

When Charles I raised his standard at Nottingham on August 22, 1642, he ignited a series of conflicts in which the English fought each other in a confusion of motives and loyalties, except perhaps for the king, who declared: "I am going to fight for my crown and my dignity." The king's decorative troops were known as Cavaliers, a name later applied to all royalist followers. The Parliament supporters were called

Roundheads; they were militant Puritans who cut their hair close to the head to show disapproval of the Cavaliers and their flowing wigs; they also raised and trained an army. The followers of Charles I came from the nobles (many of whom were Catholics), the Anglican clergy, and the peasantry, especially in northern and west-central England. His opposition came primarily from the middle classes: the great merchants and artisans in the eastern and southeastern counties, "where even the gentry were firm Puritans." The larger towns, notably the commercial centers and ports where most of the country's wealth was now concentrated, supported Parliament; they felt that their newly acquired riches had earned them a larger role in the government. Thus it was not religion so much that caused the English Civil War but the shift in economic power to the House of Commons which, said Maurice Ashley, "could buy the House of Lords three times over." It was Winston Churchill who described the Commons as a coalition of merchants, manufacturers, and tenant-farmers now "claiming a share of political power which had hitherto been almost monopolised by the aristocracy and the hereditary landlords." But as far as the parliamentary army was concerned, the war soon became a religious quarrel. To Oliver Cromwell, the Puritan squire in command of the army, "Religion was not the thing at first contested for, but God brought it to that issue at last; and ... it proved that which was most dear to us."

On religious questions, English Presbyterians and Puritans opposed not only absolute monarchy and the Anglican Church but each other. When the king's supporters withdrew from Parliament, the House of Commons was divided: the Presbyterians, ruled by a council of elders, merely wanted to limit the powers of the crown, while the Independents, or Puritan extremists, wanted that power put into the hands of elected representatives. A captain in the parliamentary army, which supported the Independents, said the question "was whether the King should govern as a god ... or whether the people should be governed by laws made by themselves."

It was inevitable that the upheaval in England, in which religious and political issues were inseparable, would make the status of Maryland's Catholic-controlled government increasingly insecure. The colony's Catholics had been instructed of course to "treate the Protestants with as much mildness and favour as Justice will permitt." Still, there was talk of a Protestant revolt. And New England Puritans, when invited to move to Maryland, refused.

The first Puritans to sail to America for religious reasons were the Pilgrims and Separatists (those who wished to abandon the Church of England), who arrived at Plymouth in 1620. They were followed by the Puritans who settled Salem in 1622 and Boston in 1630.

Puritans had migrated to Virginia as early as 1619, but it was not until war broke out in England that they were really noticed by the authorities. At that time a number of Puritan pastors arrived and began to preach throughout the colony, attracting large congregations. Within a year they were forced to leave Virginia when the assembly passed the following act:

> *For the preservation of the purity of doctrine and unity of the church, it is enacted that all ministers whatsoever, which shall reside in the colony, are to be conformable to the orders and constitutions of the Church of England and the laws therein established; and not otherwise to be admitted to teach or preach, publickly or privately; and that the governor and council do take care that all non-conformists, upon notice of them, shall be compelled to depart the colony with all convenience.*

Though their pastors were silenced publicly, the Virginia Puritans continued to hear them preach in their private homes, and Puritans would maintain a sizable presence in the colony until invited by Lord Baltimore to resettle in Maryland in 1649.

Virginia's Puritanism lacked the fervor of the Puritanism in England or New England. In Virginia, wrote Morison, it "merely reflected the average Englishman's desire to support honesty and morality, in the absence of Anglican discipline and authority." In New England it was a way of life "difficult for anyone to escape." In England, *Puritan* had evolved into a term of reproach and ridicule by opponents. For the Puritans, though they were the first to advance doctrines of political equality and individual freedom, had become so narrow in their religious zeal that they distributed pamphlets against all forms of "revelling, epicurisme, wantonese, idlenesse, dauncing, drinking, Stage-plaies, Masques, and carnall Pompe and Jollity."

While the king and his court supported the arts, particularly poets and playwrights, the Puritans, once they were in control of the government, "like their brethren in Massachusetts, concerned themselves actively with the repression of vice," wrote Churchill. The royal court was called "a nursery of lust and intemperance"; gambling and swearing were punishable by fines; drunkenness was attacked, taverns closed, dancing considered a crime, decorative clothing frowned upon; adulterers were put to death; theaters were shut and playwrights were agents of the devil; cockfighting was stopped by wringing the necks of the cocks; the Book of Common Prayer was condemned, walking the streets on Sundays (except to go to church) was punished, and Christmas celebrations were considered blasphemy. Yet many Puritans seized crown lands as their own and after Cromwell came to power, said Churchill, their reign was so tyrannical that it was "hated as no Government has ever been hated in England before or since." To the English nobility, at least, it was a self-serving government that lived up (or down) to words written earlier by the great playwright who was royalist at heart: "Though honesty be no puritan," wrote Shakespeare in *All's Well That Ends Well*.

About the only contemporary poet the Puritans did not attack was John Milton, who wrote in their defense: "I was born at a time when the virtue of my fellow citizens, far exceeding that of their progenitors in greatness of soul and vigour of enterprise, having invoked Heaven to witness the justice of their cause, and been clearly governed by its directions, has succeeded in delivering the commonwealth from the most grievous tyranny, and religion from the most ignominious degradation."

Even as Charles I was fighting for his crown and his life in England he continued to monitor the Baltimore-Claiborne situation. As erratic and contradictory as ever, he accused Lord Baltimore of being a "notorious parliamentarian" and named Claiborne treasurer of Virginia. The two antagonists were just as inconsistent. The royalist Lord Baltimore, having decided that the king's cause was hopeless, gradually transferred his allegiance to Parliament and reorganized his Catholic government on Protestant terms. The pragmatic Claiborne, now an active parliamentarian, tried to rally Kent Island settlers against Maryland authority in late 1642 by displaying a letter of support from the *king* instead of representing himself as a friend of Parliament. Though he failed on that attempt, in the following year he and a small company of Roundhead recruits would succeed in capturing the island.

Both Lord Baltimore and William Claiborne changed their colors during the English Civil War. One, a royalist and devout Catholic beholden to the crown for his possession of Maryland, was forced to patronize the Protestants and Parliament in order to keep control of the colony; the other, a beneficiary of royal grants and commissions, used his association with the Puritans to his political gain and to overthrow the Maryland government and vindicate his claim to Kent Island and other properties in the Chesapeake.

Seven

War and Plunder
1644-1649

Though Virginia ultimately acquired its reputation as the Cavalier
colony, largely through the actions of Governor Berkeley in his
passionate support of Charles I and the Church of England, Virginians
generally shared the parliamentary politics of the English merchants and
tradesmen from whose ranks many of them had come. Even the
royalists among them, unlike the king, did not seek to eliminate the
Parliament or to concentrate absolute power in the monarch.
Compromise was the rule of the day. With the colony's existence
dependent upon goods from abroad and developing markets for its own
commodities, the policy of the governor's council was to avoid
hostilities and maintain open trade with all vessels that entered
Chesapeake Bay, English or Dutch, or whether they were the king's
ships from Bristol or Parliament's ships from London. Still, any
disruptions in Virginia's economy led to quarrels, as did any religious or
political differences (which were closely related).

But, in the spring of 1644, Virginians had something else to worry
about—Opechancanough.

Sensing dissension among Virginians because of the war in England,
the eighty-year-old chief was on the warpath again. Nearly blind and so
emaciated that he had to be carried into battle on a litter,
Opechancanough decided this was his last chance to punish the English
for continued encroachment on lands of the dwindling Powhatan
confederacy. On April 17 he launched a surprise attack on the more
remote settlements, killing nearly four hundred colonists before the
governor could organize an effective resistance. It was not until June 1
that the assembly was convened to raise troops and choose William
Claiborne as the army's General and Chief Commander. Leaving
management of the campaign in Claiborne's hands, Berkeley sailed to

England to solicit assistance from the crown. He carried with him a declaration from the Virginia assembly that the king's colony would "declyne to a sodaine Ruine and Desolation" without support.

The call for help was unheeded, and fortunately unnecessary. Hale wrote that Claiborne's troops waged a rapid series of attacks against the vastly outnumbered Nansemonds, Seacocks, Warraskoyacks, and Chowanokes south of the James, "carried fire and sword among the villages and corn fields of the Chickahominies," and mustered more than three hundred soldiers for a final offensive against Opechancanough's stronghold in the Pamunkey country near the York. The campaign lasted for three weeks. Opechancanough escaped, and two years elapsed before he was captured and placed in a Jamestown stockade. There he was shot in the back by one of the guards.

Opechancanough's death ended the Powhatan confederacy. In a peace treaty drawn up in October 1646, his successor Necotowance formally ceded all Indian lands between the York and the falls on the upper James. One of the English forts built on the perimeter of this region was commanded by Lieutenant Thomas Rolfe, the son of the legendary Powhatan princess Pocahontas. Areas set aside for the Indians were repeatedly violated by English planters reaching out for new lands to cultivate. Soon, under the unrelenting pressure of colonial expansion, the ancient Powhatan people disappeared.

Meanwhile, the bloody struggle in England was not going well for Charles I. On July 2, 1644, the Battle of Marston Moor ended in victory for Oliver Cromwell's Roundheads and won the north country to the parliamentary cause.

Maryland had its own civil war. Protestant sympathy for parliament, supplemented by hatred for Catholics, proved a major setback for Lord Baltimore's plan to create a refuge where all Christians, Catholic and Protestant, might worship together in peace; he had instructed Governor Calvert to "suffer no scandall nor offence to be given to any of the Protestants." But the problem was more than Protestant antagonism; Calvert also was harassed by Jesuit demands for trade exemptions, more land, and more authority in governing the colony. Furthermore, the Puritans in Parliament were furious that a Catholic held possession to one of the colonies and insisted that the Maryland charter be revoked. Thus as Baltimore's position both in England and Maryland eroded, Calvert put control of the colony in the hands of a deputy governor and went to London to discuss these grave matters with his brother.

Though the brothers agreed it was in their best interests to pursue a policy of neutrality between the king and the Parliament, Calvert returned from England with a directive from the king's commissioners to seize any Parliament vessel found in Maryland or Virginia waters. Aside from the fear of losing his colony if he refused the commission, Lord Baltimore was lured by the promise that he and the king would share equally in the spoils. And since the assistance of the Virginia governor would be required, Berkeley was to be rewarded with two thousand pounds sterling. (Berkeley, in sympathy with the king but concerned that Virginia's existence depended upon markets abroad for its tobacco and other commodities, would refuse the offer.)

While Calvert was in England, danger was brewing in Maryland. It began in January 1644 when Richard Ingle, a tobacco trader from London, was "arrested upon highe treason to his Majestie" while his pinnace, the *Reformation*, was at Kent Island. Ingle had referred to himself as a "Captain of Gravesend for the Parliament against the King"; and there were rumors that he had declared Charles I "was no King, neither would be no King, nor could be no King, unless he did joine with the Parliament." Ingle had to be taken by force, and only through the friendship of the influential Thomas Cornwallis was he released on bail until his court appearance. Immediately he plotted his escape. Though the *Reformation* was under guard, he recaptured the ship with the aid again of Cornwallis. Once in command of his ship, the vindictive Ingle noted that one day soon he would "assault & beate downe the dwelling houses of the inhabitants of this colony." After seizing the stores of several vessels, Ingle anchored near St. Mary's to await Cornwallis.

Not only was Cornwallis forced to pay a fine of one thousand pounds of tobacco for his involvement in Ingle's escape, but he also had to pledge security for the judgement against Ingle. Then, concerned about his safety because of the sudden bitterness against him in the colony, Cornwallis placed his estate in the care of an agent, Cuthbert Fenwick, and sailed with Ingle to England.

In London, after meeting with the king's "enemies & rebels" and giving an account of his Maryland experience, Ingle was commissioned to return to Chesapeake Bay aboard the *Reformation*, now armed with twelve guns, and "take all ships and vessels with their goods and Company" that were deemed hostile to the Parliament. The commission was authorized by the Lord High Admiral of England.

When Ingle arrived in Virginia in early 1645 he stopped off at Jamestown where he heard that Calvert had returned to Maryland with royal instructions to recruit an army of royalists. He also heard that Maryland's government was now composed entirely of "papists" and that Protestant troublemakers had been disarmed and had their property confiscated. It was all the vengeful Ingle needed to set about hiring Virginians for the force he would need to overthrow the Maryland authorities. Before leaving Jamestown, he read the crew his commission from Parliament, misrepresented the *Reformation* as a man-of-war ordered to lay waste to royalist Maryland, and agreed to give the crew a sixth of the pillage. Ingle then sent an equally misleading message to the Protestant leaders in Maryland, informing them of Parliament's intent to drive the Roman Catholics from the colony and confiscate their property. Ingle's strategy worked: it won the support of the colony's parliamentarians and terrorized the royalists.

William Claiborne decided to take advantage of distractions in England and the disorder in Maryland to rally a company of about a dozen Virginia Puritans and sail up the Chesapeake to reassert his claim to Kent Island. Along the way he mustered added support from the remote settlement of Chicacoan, on the upper Virginia peninsula between the Potomac and Rappahannock Rivers. The Chicacoan planters were Kent Island refugees who considered themselves an independent community outside the jurisdiction of St. Mary's, with no particular loyalty to the distant government in Jamestown; those who joined Claiborne's campaign did so because they shared his sense of loss and retribution. Unlike the 1642 campaign that failed to recapture Kent Island, this one succeeded in inciting the islanders to rebellion because they saw that the Maryland government was too weak to retaliate. The old fort and the commander's house at Crayford were taken with little resistance, and the island was again in William Claiborne's possession.

Before the Maryland militia could respond, the governor was told that Captain Ingle's *Reformation* was approaching St. Mary's. Since Calvert had been alerted to the purpose of Ingle's visit, he was not deceived when advised that the captain was merely transporting trading supplies to Thomas Cornwallis's agent. When Ingle was informed that he was free to return to Maryland with the rights of friendly trade, he sneered at the overture and on February 1645 sailed his vessel into the river at St. Mary's and landed at a small fort defending the approach to the capital city. From there he was able to seize the Dutch merchant vessel, *Spiegel*, although it was armed with eleven guns. And despite the fact the *Spiegel* had been chartered by London merchants in sympathy with Parliament, Ingle justified the seizure by claiming he feared the ship would be used against him. Now, with two heavily armed vessels under his command, Ingle attacked St. Mary's and took as prisoners many of the colony's top officials. Calvert, however, fled to Virginia.

Ingle and his men went on a rampage that continued for nearly two years, pillaging and destroying property throughout the colony, including the manor house of the man whom he claimed "had saved his life" when he was apprehended in 1644: the Cornwallis estate was stripped of everything of value—from silverware and tapestries to the furs, tobacco, and other commodities Ingle was supposed to protect; even the servants and slaves were taken aboard his two ships. Storehouses were looted, government buildings and official records were put to the torch, the Great Seal of Maryland was lost, nothing was spared. And all through this reign of terror and anarchy which has come to be known as *the plundering time*, Ingle's every whim became law. Marylanders were forced to swear an oath against Lord Baltimore and the king; when the Catholics refused, many were persecuted, some found sanctuary in Virginia. But Ingle's Protestant followers were rewarded, under the guise of improving the lot of those settlers who had been disadvantaged because of their loyalty to Parliament. Father White was among the many prominent prisoners herded aboard the *Reformation* for transport to England. By the time Ingle departed Maryland in 1646, leaving the colony without a government and taking the *Spiegle* as a prize, the population had been reduced to one hundred settlers.

Calvert, leading his exiled Marylanders and an armed force furnished by Virginia's apprehensive Governor Berkeley, crossed the Potomac in December 1646 unopposed. At St. Mary's he reestablished his authority over the Protestant rebels scattered along Maryland's western shoreline. But worried about the delicate political situation in England, Calvert found it expedient to pardon anyone who had engaged in the rebellion if he acknowledged "sorrow for his act ... before the feast of St. Michael the Archangell next."

Claiborne, isolated and unprotected on an island now in ruins, and lacking sanctions from the Virginia government for his militant actions, returned to Jamestown to resume his responsibilities as the colony's Treasurer. In that role he was viewed suspiciously by Berkeley who considered him disloyal to Charles I and a parliamentarian threat to his governor's seat. Berkeley was right in all but one particular: Claiborne did support the goals of the Parliament cause and was pragmatic in using the cause to advance his personal aims, but he tried to remain faithful to the king who had granted his Chesapeake Bay trading rights and to whom he owed his position and property in Virginia.

As to his involvement in the devastation of Maryland, there is no evidence of collusion between Claiborne and Ingle. The consensus is that Claiborne's association with Ingle was incidental, that he was not personally involved in the plundering but merely used the situation to recover Kent Island.

Once Ingle was back in England, he defended his raid on Thomas Cornwallis's estate by accusing his benefactor of being an enemy to Parliament and succeeded in having him imprisoned. Ingle's justification, after branding Cornwallis a papist, was to explain to the Puritan judges that he had used the spoils to relieve "the poore distressed Protestants there whoe otherwise must have starved and been rooted out." As soon as friends arranged his release, Cornwallis sued the unscrupulous captain demanding compensation for his stolen valuables and trading goods.

On March 26, 1646, England's Civil War ended in victory for Cromwell's parliamentary army at Stowe-on-the-Wold. Charles I took refuge in Scotland but remained at risk; in January 1647 the Scots surrendered him to Parliament in return for 400,000 pounds. Within months, the victors were in a power struggle: The army refused to accede to an act of Parliament to disband, seized the king and made him a prisoner, then tried to coerce the Parliament into backing Cromwell as England's guardian.

Claiborne, who would benefit from the events in England, added to his holdings in 1647 with the acquisition of seven hundred acres situated in the old Kecoughtan settlement, bordered on the west by Southampton River, on the east by Chesapeake Bay, and on the south by the great harbor (today's Hampton Roads). Actually, the land had been granted to his wife for transporting fourteen persons to the colony. Had Claiborne been a less ambitious man he might have been content with his standing in the colony and his Virginia holdings, which by this time amounted to five thousand acres. But as it became more and more apparent that the Parliament would revoke Lord Baltimore's Maryland charter, Claiborne busied himself gathering the documents he would need to press his claim to the upper Chesapeake.

At that time his writings repeated a familiar theme: "Wee clearly claime right by possession haveing planted the Ile of Kent almost three years before ever the name of Maryland was heard of, and Burgesses for that place setting in the Assembly of Virginia whereby it is evident that the Lord of Baltamores suggestion to the king that those parts were uncultivated and unplanted, unlesse by barbarous people not haveing knowledge of God, was a misinformation, and by it that Patent appeares illegally gotten." Had King James or King Charles been better advised, wrote Claiborne, they would not "have granted such a Patent as this of Maryland, it being neer two third parts of the better Territory of Virginia [a gross exaggeration]; and as no way consistent with Equity, and the Honor and publick Faith of the Kingdom ... and most injurious to the Rights and Interests of the noble Adventurers [investors] and the painful indefatigable Planters, who had so long under God, conserved the Countrey from total ruine."

To Claiborne, religion alone should have disqualified Lord Baltimore's charter:

> *Why therefore should Maryland, so ill Founded, and so ill Managed, be wrung from the right of Virginia, against all Law and Equity, as is before truely set forth? And be established to Lord Baltamore, a professed Recusant, as his publish'd Book intimates; who hath in effect made it a subject of his own domination and tyranny (being his main aim) But to colour it, and the better to get friends, first made it a receptacle for Papists, and Priests, and Jesuites, in some extraordinary and zealous maner, but hath since discontented them many times and many ways, though Intelligence with Bulls, Letters, etc. from the Pope and Rome be ordinary for his own Interests; and now admitts all sorts of Religions, and intended even 2000 Irish, and by his own Letters clears and indemnifies one, that said, Those Irish would not leave a Bible in Maryland. His Countrey, till he employed Captain Stone, never had but Papist Governours and Counsellors, dedicated to St. Ignatius, as they call him, and his Chappel and Holyday kept solemnly: The Protestants for the most time miserably disturbed in the exercise of their Religion, by many wayes plainly enforced, or by subtil practises, or hope of preferment, to turn Papists, of which a very sad account may from time to time be given, even from their first arrivall, to this very day.*

Claiborne was saddened by news that Swedish and Dutch colonies had usurped lands clearly within Virginia's original territorial boundaries and were carrying on a profitable trade in furs which he could have controlled had it not been for Lord Baltimore.

Always alert to the danger of Claiborne's return, Maryland authorities announced that anyone assisting him in his attempts to take "the Island of Kent, or any place within this Province" would be punished by death. It turned out to be a threat with no bite. That Maryland's end was near seemed inevitable when Leonard Calvert died in June 1647.

On his deathbed, Calvert had named Thomas Greene, a Catholic and royalist, to succeed him as governor. But Lord Baltimore, sensitive to the times, removed Greene and appointed Captain William Stone, a Protestant living in Virginia. He also made certain that the majority of his councillors were Protestants. It was a move that temporarily dampened Claiborne's hopes of recovering his Chesapeake possessions; that is, until Stone and the councillors were forced to swear that they would not "molest any person in the colony professing to believe in Jesus Christ ... in particular no Roman Catholic."

In November 1647 Charles I escaped from prison and signed a secret treaty with the Scots who promised to restore his throne by force upon his agreement to restore Presbyterianism to Scotland. The conspiracy set off an Anglo-Scottish war which ended on August 20, 1648, when Cromwell's army defeated the Scots in the Battle of Preston. Following revelations of the secret treaty, Parliament renounced its allegiance to Charles I and in December brought the king to trial. "We will cut off the king's head with the crown on it," trumpeted Oliver Cromwell, who saw it as an act of conscience.

Charles I, after denying the jurisdiction of the court that sentenced him to death, was beheaded on January 30, 1649. Though his son was proclaimed Charles II in Scotland, in parts of Ireland, and in the Channel Islands, England was declared "a Commonwealth or Free State." The House of Commons, in concert with Oliver Cromwell and his army, had resolved that "the Commons of England in Parliament assembled, being chosen by and representing the people, have the supreme power in this nation." Scratched on the pedestal bearing a broken statue of Charles I were the words: "Exit the tyrant, the last of the Kings." England would be governed from 1649 to 1660 without a monarch.

In most of those eleven years, William Claiborne would hold the upper hand in his struggle with Lord Baltimore.

Eight

Victory in Compromise
1649-1660

In 1649 the Puritans in Virginia were being harassed by Governor Berkeley and his inflexible royalists who had ignored Parliament's victory and cast their lot with "the late King's eldest Sonne." Led by Richard Bennett, a former member of the Virginia council, some five hundred of the Puritans abandoned their homes and resettled in Maryland at the invitation of the colony's new Protestant governor.

What attracted the Puritans to this Catholic stronghold was *An Act Concerning Religion*, better known as the famous Toleration Act of 1649, passed by the Maryland assembly following the appointment of William Stone. To maintain "mutuall Love and amity amongst the Inhabitants," the act declared that

> *noe person or persons whatsoever within this Province, or the Islands, Ports, Harbors, Creekes, or havens thereunto belonging professing to believe in Jesus Christ, shall from henceforth bee any waies troubled, Molested or discountenanced for or in respect of his or her religion nor in the free exercise thereof within this Province or the Ilands thereunto belonging nor any way compelled to the beliefe or exercise of any other Religion against his or her consent, soe as they bee not unfaithfull to the Lord Proprietary, or molest or conspire against the civill Government established or to bee established in this Province under him or his heires.*

The act punished anyone who called another person "an heretick, Scismatick, Idolator, puritan, Independent, Prespiterian popish prest, Jesuite, Jesuited papist, Lutheran, Calvenist, Anabaptist, Brownist, Antinomian, Barrowist, Roundhead, Separatist, or any other name or terme in a reproachfull manner relating to matter of Religion." Thus its intent was not only to protect Catholics but also to protect Maryland against charges that it was purely a Roman Catholic colony. The religious toleration it proclaimed, however, was limited, excluding

Jews, Unitarians, and other non-Christians. Though it has been described as merely another of Lord Baltimore's moves to save his charter, the Toleration Act of 1649 was preceded by the Baltimore policy dating back to November 1633, instructing Governor Calvert and the Maryland commissioners "to bee very careful to do justice to every man without partiality."

The Puritans settled a site on the Severn River they called Providence (which one day would be renamed Annapolis and become Maryland's capital city). Agitated by William Claiborne, according to most Maryland historians, they refused to acknowledge Baltimore as "absolute lord" as required by the oath. Instead they inserted a condition declaring that the oath was "not in any wise understood to infringe or prejudice liberty of conscience."

On April 19, 1650, the general assembly took another stand against Claiborne's invasion of Maryland affairs, passing an act "prohibiting all complyance with Captain Cleyborne":

> *Whereas Capt. Willm Cleyborne heretofore of the Ile of Kent within this Province of Maryland and nowe of the Collony of Virginia for his frequent Attempts practizes and enterprizes in opposicion of his Lordshipps undoubted right and Dominion in and over this Province hath heretofore carryed himself in a very rebellious manner against his Lordshipp and the Government here established under him, and still remaines exempt from pardon in that respect.*

It was held also that on April 4, 1639, "before the Lords of the Counsell in England, the said Cleybornes pretended clayme to the said Ile of Kent and some other parts of his Lordshipps Province and trade with the Indians was rejected and his Lordshipps undoubted right and title thereunto according to his Patent was confirmed."

Furthermore, the April 19 assembly noted that Claiborne and all other inhabitants of Virginia had been "expresly prohibited [by the Virginia governor and council] to use or exercize any trade or commerce with any Indians within the Bounds of his Lordshipps Province without special Licence from his Lordshipp for that purpose uppon the penalty & forfeiture therein expressed."

Claiborne was accused of declaring "in speeches that hee purposeth ere long to make some attempt uppon the Ile of Kent against the peace & safety of this Province for prevencion whereof therefore and the better to restraine and keepe all & every the Inhabitants of this Province in their due obedience to his Lordshipp and the Government established here under him."

Finally, it was enacted that anyone who might "assist abett or countenance the said Cleyborne or any of his Complices or Adherents in any attempt practize or enterprize whatsoever uppon or against the said Iland of Kent or any other place within this Province" or in any opposition to Lord Baltimore and his heirs "shalbe punished by death & confiscacion of all his and theire Lands goods Debts & chattells within this Province."

Also passed in 1649 was an act punishing "certaine Offences as Swearing, cursing, Adultery, etc.," the penalty being "100 pounds tobacco paid to the Lord Proprietary." At the same time, there was an order for "the releife of the poore."

There was an act "prohibiting any Indians to come into Kent or Annarundell Counties without notice thereof given." A year earlier, the assembly had declared that "Noe Inhabitant of this Province shall deliver any Gunns or Ammunition to any Pagan for the killing of meate or to any other use uppon payne of forfeiture to the Lord Proprietary 1000lb tobacco and loss of the partyes Gunn to him that shall make seizure thereof or take the same from such Pagan or to him that shall informe thereof and able to make proofe thereof."

An Act of Oblivion was "enacted by the said Lord Proprietary with the consent of the upper and lower house of this Assembly that there shall bee an utter Abolition of all actions tending to recover dammages for any faulte committed against anyone in his Lordshipps peace by any of the party who were in Rebellion against his Lordshipps Government here att any tyme betweene the 15th of February 1644 and the 5th of August 1646 excepting Richard Ingle and John Danford Marryners and such others of the Ile of Kent as were not pardoned by his Lordshipps Brother Leonard Calvert Esquire deceased his Lordshipps late Lieuetenant of this Province."

Since Baltimore had maintained control of Maryland at the pleasure of the crown, his policy of coddling Puritans angered Charles II who, even in exile, attempted to invalidate the charter. It was an empty gesture and one which Baltimore believed would support his loyalty to the commonwealth. But he could not overcome his Catholic background with the Puritans in England or even those in Maryland who sent a delegation to London to join the opposition in Parliament to his possession of the colony.

Virginians made no attempt to conceal their loyalty to the exiled king and had to be reminded that they were "subject to such laws and regulations as are or shall be made by Parliament."

In October 1650 Parliament created a commission with the power to reduce Virginia (and Maryland *as part of Virginia*, along with Barbadoes, Antigua, and Bermuda) to subjection. Four commissioners were named but only two would exercise any control: Richard Bennett and William Claiborne. It was their responsibility to establish in each of the colonies a new government built on the principles of the English Commonwealth. Though Lord Baltimore tried to have his province exempted, Maryland was emphasized in a new phrase (added by Claiborne) urging the commissioners "to use their best endeavors to reduce all the plantations within the Bay of Chesopiack to their due obedience to the Parliament of England." Their best endeavors would be backed by an armed fleet.

Governor Berkeley, in a foolish attempt to resist Parliament's instructions, mustered the Virginia militia and engaged the aid of a few Dutch ships anchored in Chesapeake Bay. Virginia's council and assembly overruled the governor and forced him to agree to the laws and wishes of Parliament. Berkeley was then given amnesty for his actions and allowed to retire to his Virginia plantation, which became a sanctuary for England's Cavalier refugees.

Next, Bennett and Claiborne sailed up the bay to St. Mary's to receive the surrender of Maryland from Governor Stone, who, after an appeal by Maryland inhabitants, was permitted to remain as head of the government under the watchful eye of a new Puritan assembly which repudiated all authority of Lord Baltimore.

On their return to Jamestown, the commissioners were informed that Parliament had appointed Bennett to serve as Virginia's new governor and Claiborne as its secretary of state. Members of the General Assembly were granted the power to elect all of the other officials, and no taxes were to be levied without their consent. Thus Virginia, the last of the colonies to abandon the monarchy, entered upon a period of almost complete self-government under the protection of the English Commonwealth. Both Maryland and Virginia would enjoy more prosperity and freedom under parliamentary rule than they had known under the crown—and Claiborne would strengthen his claim to his Chesapeake properties. In the Virginia Articles of Surrender, he and Bennett promised (but never delivered) a restoration of "the antient bounds and lymitts" that would place Kent and the other islands within Virginia's jurisdiction.

Claiborne's signature appeared with Bennett's on a pass which authorized Colonel Francis Lovelace to deliver to Parliament news of "ye reducement of this Collony of Virginia." An armorial seal appeared next to Claiborne's signature, the only instance he used the coat of arms of the ancient Cliburns of Westmoreland County, England.

At last, Claiborne "could be revenged for the many injustices which he felt had been done him," wrote Raphael Semmes; yet "he did nothing to avenge the wrongs he had suffered." There is nothing in the Maryland records to indicate that Claiborne was personally involved in any destructive actions or any plunder in the colony. He was no Richard Ingle.

Of course, in view of Claiborne's ardent support of "the Keepers of the Liberties of England" after the fall of Charles I, not everyone has shared Semmes's high opinion of his character. Perhaps not surprising, in *Maryland the Land of Sanctuary*, Father W. T. Russell wrote: "So sudden a change of politics was of little concern to him. Episcopalian, abettor of Puritans, Royalist, or Parliamentarian, he was capable of being almost anything but a friend of Lord Baltimore's and an honest man." To Clayton C. Hall, in *The Lords Baltimore and the Maryland Palatinate*, "No politician, ancient or modern, could change face quicker." William Hand Browne, in his *History of Maryland*, wished that Claiborne had "sailed under fewer flags." He has been described as both "the Bane of Maryland" and "the Evil Genius of Maryland," as "an unprincipled incendiary" and a man "feeding the fires of Puritan arrogance and desire." He was "a pestilent enemie" to John Hammond who, in "A word to the Governour and Counsell in Virginia," wrote: "I cannot except nor speake against any of ye, but Will. Claiborne, whom you all know to be a Villaine, but it is no more blemish to your degree, to have him of your society, then it was to the Apostles to have Judas of theirs."

Yet he has been called "worthy of honour and respect [as] the first actual settler of the territory of Maryland." Campbell saw him as Virginia's "Champion and Defender." J. H. Latane, author of *Early Relations of Virginia and Maryland*, said that "we cannot help recognizing the strength of Claiborne's claims and admiring the resolution and persistency with which he defended them." Claiborne, slightly overstating the case, declared that he was "wronged with as grievous oppressions as ever Englishmen endured at the hands of their countrymen."

Less than four years after the conclusion of England's Civil War, the nation was at war with the Dutch, a sister republic which for many years had been defended by English troops against Spain. Now, in 1651, primarily because the Dutch controlled most of the colonial trade shipments, Parliament passed the first in a series of Navigation Acts prohibiting the importation of goods into the Commonwealth except in English ships or ships owned by the country producing the goods. Foreign vessels were forbidden to trade with the English colonies except under license from the Parliament or the Council of State; the purpose was "to hinder the carrying over of any such persons as are enemies to this Commonwealth, or that may prove dangerous to any of the English plantations in America." Although the act was all but ignored by the colonies, it did restrict Dutch commerce until hostilities ended in April 1654.

The war also disrupted the Parliament's conduct of the Commonwealth and weakened its opposition to Oliver Cromwell who took over the government in 1653 with no resistance. Accompanied by thirty musketeers, Cromwell cleared Parliament of its members, declaring, "I will put an end to your prating. You are no Parliament." He then replaced the Commonwealth with a Protectorate, naming himself Lord Protector of England, Scotland, and Ireland. Though "hugely taken" with the idea of becoming king, he backed off when the army showed its "hostility to the trappings of monarchy." It made little difference; for the next five years he would rule as a dictator.

Lord Baltimore welcomed Cromwell's new government, convinced that it would terminate the restrictions that Parliament had placed on the colonies. In viewing the change as an opportunity to restore the authority revoked by Maryland's Puritan-controlled assembly, he issued a proclamation commanding Governor Stone and his Catholic-controlled council to seize the property of all those who had not taken the oath of fidelity to Baltimore as lord proprietor. When the Maryland Puritans still refused on the grounds that the oath violated their allegiance to the Commonwealth, they were declared rebels to Lord Baltimore.

To resolve the matter, Parliament dispatched Bennett and Claiborne to Maryland with orders to oust Stone and install a government that would be managed in the name of the Lord Protector. William Fuller, serving as temporary governor, instructed the general assembly to pass an Act of Recognition, whereby it would declare "in the Name of his Highness the Lord Protector of England Scotland and Ireland and the Dominions thereunto belonging and the Authority of this present General Assembly, That the Reduceing of this Province of Maryland by power of the Supreame Authority of the Commonwealth of England [is] Committed to Richard Bennett Esqr and Coll. William Cleyborne."

Moreover, the assembly ruled "that no power either from the Lord Baltemore or any other ought or shall make any alteration in the Government aforesaid as it is now Settled, unless it be from the Supreame Authority of the Commonwealth of England exercized by his highness the Lord Protector, Imediately & Directly Granted for that purpose."

Next, the assembly passed an act denying protection to those of the Catholic religion. It declared "in the Name of his Highness the Lord Protector with the Consent and by the Authority of the present General Assembly that none who profess and Exercize the Popish Religion Commonly known by the Name of the Roman Catholick Religion can be protected in this Province by the Lawes of England formerly Established and yet unrepealed nor by the Government of the Commonwealth of England Scotland and Ireland and the Dominions thereunto belonging Published by his Highness the Lord protector but are to be restrained from the Exercize thereof." All other Christians would be protected in the profession of their faith and exercise of their religion so long as "they abuse not this Liberty to the injury of others."

Again, Maryland found itself engaged in a bloody rebellion. This time the victory went to the Puritans, or as Lord Baltimore's forces called them, "the Roundhead Rogues and Dogs." Twenty were slain. Among the wounded was Governor Stone who was imprisoned; four of his followers were executed. Claiborne wrote that it was "notoriously known that all of the Lord Baltamores Governors usually took the Kings part against the Parliament" and that Maryland officials allowed the "Dutch, French, or Italian Descents to plant and enjoy equal privileges with the British and Irish Nations."

The case against Baltimore was published in Maryland on July 15, 1654, and signed by Bennett and Claiborne. Governor Stone and his council were charged with failure to abide by the platform of the government of the Commonwealth

> ... *having lately Associated unto them divers Counsellors, all of the Romish Religion, and excluding others appointed by the Parliaments Commissioners, have, and do refuse to bee obedient to the Constitutions thereof, and to the Lord Protector therein; And have in name, and by special direction of the said Lord Baltamore, made Proclamation, and exacted an Oath of Fidelity from all the Inhabitants of the Province, contrary, and inconsistent to the said Platform of Government ... And whereas the said Oath, in many particulars, is distasted by all the Inhabitants of Maryland: and especially out of tenderness of Conscience by all Northern*

Plantations of Patuxent and Severne, who having lately engaged to the Parliament of England, do say, and declare, they cannot take the said Oath to the Lord Baltamore to bee absolute Lord and Proprietary of Maryland ... Uppon which their refusal of the said Oath, the said Captain Stone, by the said Lord Baltamores especial direction, hath set forth a Proclamation, declaring, That all such persons so refusing, shall bee for ever debarred from any Right, or Claim to the Lands they now enjoy, and live on ...

By which strange, and exorbitant proceedings, many great Cruelties, and Mischiefs are likely to bee committed, and many hundreds, with their Wives and Families, are utterly ruined, as hath been formerly done here, and at Kent, though Planted before the Lord Baltamores Claim to Maryland; with many Murders, and illegal Executions of men, Confiscacions of Estates and Goods, and great miseries sustained by Women and Orphans ...

Wee therefore the Commissioners of the Parliament, having written and proposed to the said Captain Stone and that Councell, for a Meeting, to procure a right understanding in the matters aforesaid, and to prevent the great inconveniences likely to ensue: In Answer thereunto, though they acknowledge our Lines Peaceable, yet so exulcerated are their minds, that in the very next Line they add, Wee in plain terms say, Wee suppose you to bee Wolves in Sheeps clothing; *with many other following like uncivil, and uncomely words, and expressions ...*

Wherefore wee advise and in the Name of his Highness the Lord Protector Require all the Inhabitants of this Province to take notice of the Premises, and to contain, and keep themselves in their due obedience under his Highness the Lord Protector of England Scotland and Ireland and the Dominions thereto belonging, of which this is undoubtedly a part, and ought to bee Governed accordingly; whereby they may assure themselves of the peaceable enjoyment of their Liberties, profession of their Religion, and their Estates, and that they shall be protected from wrong and violence in what kind soever. Hereby also Protesting against the said Captain William Stone, Mr. Thomas Hatton, and all others any way Confederate, or Assistant with them in their unlawful practises, that they may bee accomptable, and answerable to God and the State of England under his Highness the Lord Protector, for all the mischiefs, damages, losses, and disorders that may, or shall happen thereby.

On July 20 the Protestant William Stone officially resigned as the governor of Catholic Maryland. His resignation read in part:

... And whereas upon my Compliance with his Lordshipps Commands therein, not any wayes contradictory, so far as I understand, to any Command from the Supreame Authority in England, the said Commissioners, in persuance of their Declarations lately here published, have threatened, and gone about by force of Arms to compel me to decline his, the said Lord Proprietaries, Directions and Commands before mentioned; which in regard of the trust reposed in me, by his said Lordship, as Governor here under him, I conceive I was engaged not to do; I have therefore thought fit, for prevention of the effusion of Blood, and ruine of the Country and Inhabitants, by an Hostile Contest upon this occasion, to lay down my Power as Governor of this Province under his Lordship; and do promise for the future, to submit to such Government as shall be set over us by the said commissioners, in the Name, and under the Authority of his Highness the Lord Protector.

Bennett and Claiborne appointed ten commissioners to succeed the governor; they were to be responsible for "Ordering, Directing, and Governing the Affairs of Maryland, under his Highness the Lord Protector ... in his Name only, and no other; and to proceed therein as they shall see cause, and as neer as may be, according to the Laws of England." Now that Lord Baltimore was no longer in command, membership in Maryland's general assembly was denied to anyone who had taken up "Arms in War against the Parliament, or do profess the Roman Catholick Religion."

Maryland and Virginia having conformed at last to the demands of the commission created by Parliament in 1650, the two colonies were at peace and the work of Bennett and Claiborne was done.

In October 1654 the Maryland assembly passed an act "concerning Drunkeness," an act "concerning false Reports Slandering and Tale bearing," an act "concerning the Sabboth Day," and an act "concerning the Killing of Wolves [whereby] everyone who shall Kill a Wolfe and bring the head thereof to any of the Commissioners shalbe allowed one hundred pounds of tobacco from the County where the wolfe shall be killed & that such Commissioners to whom the wolves head shalbe brought shall Cutt out the Tongue of the said head to prevent that deceit of twice or oftener payment for the same head."

The assembly repealed acts "concerning Religion, Attachments & Executions, deserted plantations and Seatings, Mutinies & Seditious Speeches," and an act "concerning Coll. Cleyborne."

In 1655 the Virginia assembly elected a new governor: Bennett was succeeded by Edward Digges. The assembly also enacted legislation that allowed all "free men" the right to vote for burgesses, on the grounds that it was hard to reason why men who paid taxes would have no representation. Other reforms included a prohibition on taking Indian lands and the admission of ships from all nations into Virginia ports. A year later, Digges was replaced by William Claiborne's friend and supporter, Samuel Matthews, who had recently served as Virginia's agent at the Protectorate court in London.

By the end of 1657 there was change again in Maryland. Lord Baltimore pledged his loyalty to the Protectorate and persuaded the committee of trade in London to restore all of his privileges under the original charter. Baltimore offered as proof of his allegiance the reminder that Charles I had disclaimed him for granting asylum to the Puritans chased out of Virginia. He also was pressured to withdraw his edicts against Claiborne. On regaining his authority, Baltimore appointed his son Philip Calvert as the new governor.

Oliver Cromwell died in the autumn of 1658 at age fifty-nine. Historians have given his reign harsh reviews. To Churchill, he was "a reluctant and apologetic dictator." Maurice Ashley said that he "died hated by all save a few intimate friends and admirers." To Charles Carlton, Cromwell's villainy could be justified in "the sincere belief" that he was right; or as he himself would say, by his principle of "liberty of conscience." He perhaps considered himself a tolerant ruler who held to a narrow definition of liberty or freedom (Roman Catholics need not apply)—influenced on the one side by radical Puritan sects like the Fifth Monarchy Men, which believed the Second Coming of Christ was at hand, and on the other by such men as James Harrington, who taught that the ideal society was dependent on the "direct relationship between the distribution of property and political power." Whatever positive impact he may have had on the English commonwealth was soon squandered in the ineffectiveness of his successor, his son Richard, who proved to be so weak that the army quickly seized control of the government.

Yet military rule was not a solution to the anarchy which threatened to drive the nation into another rebellion; weary of constitutional debate, the army leaders finally called a "free parliament"—one whose membership now included many of the royal supporters. Soon it was conceded that the only way to stabilize the realm was to restore the monarchy. By act of Parliament, the son of Charles I was recalled from exile, and on May 29, 1660, he was crowned Charles II.

Restored with the king and both houses of Parliament was the Church of England, though a touch of Puritanism would soften its Episcopalian ritual. Like most wars, this struggle might have been avoided had the crown and the English church been less rigid toward Puritan demands that were not all that excessive. Then again, in what appeared to be a victory for monarchy, lessons were learned. Everyone, said Churchill, "now took it for granted that the Crown was the instrument of Parliament and the King the servant of the people." The English Civil War assured the emergence of the middle class, enlarged the influence of the mercantile community, aided religious tolerance, resolved the conflict between the crown and Parliament. Never again would the English people be victims of raw power without the rule of law, except of course in the colonies.

But for now the colonies too rejoiced.

During the strife between Charles I and Parliament, and the chaos that continued throughout the rule by Parliament and then by Cromwell, England was too occupied with survival to show any real interest in colonization. But conditions, attitudes, and ambitions changed after the coronation of Charles II. Support for overseas ventures resurfaced among English merchants and investors anxious to make up for lost time and reap the huge profits they anticipated through expansion. For the king, colonization offered a chance to pay off the political debts he had incurred during his struggle to gain the throne, chiefly through land grants and trade monopolies that could be awarded to his most devoted followers; his economic debts could be paid off through the increased revenues resulting from the expansion and development of American colonies.

Thus the need for income led not only to an increase in the number of new colonies chartered in America but also made it imperative to make existing colonies more productive. The fact that Lord Baltimore had earlier shown his talent for turning a profit must have improved his claim to Maryland, along with the return to power of his well-connected friends. For soon after Charles II was declared king, Baltimore obtained royal letters supporting his proprietary government and voiding laws enacted against Maryland under the authority of Parliament. Governor Philip Calvert was succeeded by his twenty-three-year-old brother Charles.

All but one Virginian were reconciled that Maryland's charter was restored for all time.

Following the restoration of the Calverts, the indentured population of Maryland was revitalized, with a significant increase among women. George Alsop offered this report in his 1666 account, *A Character of the Province of Maryland:*

> The Women that go over into this Province as Servants, have the best luck here as in any place of the world besides; for they are no sooner on shoar, but they are courted into a Copulative Matrimony, which some of them (for aught I know) had they not come to such a Market with their Virginity, might have kept it by them until it had been mouldy, unless they had let it out by a yearly rent to some of the Inhabitants of Lewknors-lane [a disreputable neighborhood in London], or made a Deed of Gift of it to Mother Coney, having only a poor stipend out of it, until the Gallows or Hospital called them away.

As to Maryland's male servants, Alsop wrote:

> Men have not altogether so good luck as Women in this kind, or natural preferment, without they be good Rhetoricians, and well vers'd in the Art of perswasion, then (probably) they may ryvet themselves in the time of their Servitude into the private and reserved favour of their Mistress, if Age speak their Master deficient.

The immigration increase also rendered a change in Maryland's religious composition. By 1660, the colony that had started out as a sanctuary for Catholics was predominantly Protestant. That the Catholics continued to control most of the power and prestige did not diminish Lord Baltimore's experiment in tolerance. As Morison wrote, no other Roman Catholic colony, whether Spanish, French, or Portuguese, permitted Protestants "to exist, much less acquire land and hold office." Not only should high credit go to Baltimore, he added, but also to the English government "which allowed and even encouraged Roman Catholics to live in Maryland without the disabilities under which they suffered at home." The Maryland experiment would become "one of the cornerstones of the American republic."

About the time that Charles II was being proclaimed king, Samuel Matthews died and the Virginia assembly immediately sought the return of a "royal" governor. The most likely candidate was Sir William Berkeley, the former governor who had refused to surrender to the Commonwealth and its appointed commissioners. Now he named one of those commissioners to his council. William Claiborne, to leave no doubt that he had cast aside his Commonwealth allegiance, accepted the royal commission as Virginia's secretary of state.

Perhaps what ultimately emerged from the decade of the 1650s, in the local experience of William Claiborne and Lord Baltimore as well as the larger developments in England, was a kind of victory in compromise.

Nine

Final Appeal

Virginia's boundaries continued to shrink in 1662 when a new Carolina charter (voiding all previous patents) was granted to the Earl of Clarendon, the king's chief minister, and other notables. The charter included still more of the territory granted to the original Virginia Company. But since there had been no permanent settlement in the region following the revocation of the company charter in 1624, the territory was subject to the disposal of the crown. In today's vernacular, it was *deja vu* all over again.

While Virginia was losing territory, the decade of the 1650s had been generous to Claiborne, not alone in political power but his property holdings had increased to the point that he was now a legitimate member of the colony's landed gentry. Between 1651 and 1653 he acquired nearly six thousand acres in Northumberland County, the northern neck of Virginia where the Potomac empties into Chesapeake Bay. Also in 1653, he was granted five thousand acres north of the York along the Pamunkey River, to which he soon added sixteen hundred acres; the tract fell into an area which, within a year, would be set off as New Kent County, carved out of upper York County by an act of the Virginia assembly. New Kent, of course, was named by Claiborne.

When succeeded as Virginia's secretary of state by Thomas Ludwell in 1661, Claiborne retired with Elizabeth and their three sons, Thomas, Leonard, and John, to New Kent County. There, over-looking the Pamunkey River, he had built a splendid manor called Romancoke (the Indian word he had applied to an early Kent Island plantation). No description exists, but Romancoke must have been similar to the estate of his close friend Samuel Matthews which, according to Campbell, was representative of Virginia plantations of that period. There would have been expansive lawns, shade trees, hedges, and formal gardens; stables, barns, and a carriage house. Slaves would clear and cultivate the land for tobacco, wheat, and other commodities. A number of indentured servants would be trained in a variety of trades. Typically, Claiborne would sow his own flax and manufacture his own linen, maintain a tannery and blacksmith shop, have his own carpenters, weavers, and shoemakers. The manor would include hogs and poultry, a dairy, a herd of cows and horses. A deep water dock would accommodate vessels trading in the colony, and he may well have built his own boats, as he did at Kent Island. Claiborne received most of the New Kent acreage under the headright system for transporting a hundred or more persons to Virginia, of whom many appeared among names in the Kent Island records. Not far from Romancoke lived William Jr. with his wife, also named Elizabeth, and their son William III. Daughter Jane and her husband Thomas Brereton of Northumberland County soon would settle in New Kent.

William Jr., elected New Kent representative in the general assembly from 1663 to 1666, was active in Jamestown politics. Like his father, he would serve with distinction as a military commander in campaigns against the Indians that were pillaging plantations above the York River. A citation, recorded at New Kent in 1677, included the following tribute:

> *Collo. William Clayborne Jun. hath given testimony of all the World of his singular Courage, Prudence and most remarkable loyalty to his Majesty and his Governor of Virginia as well as in his Service against the Indians as against the late Rebellion not regarding the hazard of his person or his estates so that he might promote his Majesty's and Country's Service which for the encouragement of those do justice to his merits and good Deservings...*

The citation was signed by Governor William Berkeley.

William's second son Thomas became a Lieutenant Colonel in the Virginia militia and married Sara Fenn, the daughter of Samuel and Dorothy Fenn of Middle Plantation (Williamsburg); their son Thomas would marry the great granddaughter of Claiborne's old friend John West, a son of Lord Delawarr, Virginia's first governor.

Leonard was an adventurer who settled in Spanish-owned Jamaica with his wife and two daughters. He died there in 1694. Concerning Leonard, Claiborne biographer John Esten Cooke offered this highly fanciful explanation for the rivalry between the Claibornes and the Calverts: William's older brother Thomas had competed with Cecil Calvert for the hand of the highborn Frances Lowther. When Cecil, the "young Lochinvar who came out of the west," lost, the Calverts, "from that time forth, swore enmity to the clan of Claiborne." While there is no evidence to support the tale, Maryland historian Decourcy Thom did wonder whether he heard "the rustle of a skirt." He found it curious that William Claiborne gave his son Leonard "the name of his deadly enemy," the Leonard Calvert who was the first to govern Maryland. Since Torrence later found that the name of Thomas's widow was *Jane* rather than Frances, and since there was a Calvert estate in North Yorkshire not far from Cliburn Hall, it appears that Cooke may have made the same mistake as other writers who have traced William Claiborne's direct descent to northwestern England instead of to Kent County in the east.

Eventually Claiborne's Pamunkey acreage in New Kent would be divided among three of the sons, with the Romancoke mansion house going to the eldest, William Jr. Thomas's land would become known as *Sweet Hall* and John's would be known as *Cohoke*.

Claiborne's enemy for more than forty years, Cecil Calvert, second Lord Baltimore, died on November 30, 1675. Though he and his heirs would create a fortune from titles, land patents, and monopolies bestowed upon them as royal favorites, Cecil was seen as "a greathearted far-sighted nobleman endowed with good common sense," an "Absolute Lord" whose behavior toward his Marylanders was evenhanded and respectful—traits which one historian found surprising in "an environment of greed, self-seeking, and corruption."

Cecil was succeeded to the sole proprietorship of Maryland by his son Charles Calvert, who personally governed the colony for a period of five years. In 1684, as the third Lord Baltimore, he returned to England to settle a border dispute with William Penn, whose province had once been part of the Swedish colony settled in 1638 at Fort Christiana (now Wilmington). Conquered by the Dutch in 1655 and annexed to New Netherlands (now New York), the land was then seized by the English in 1664 and became the domain of the Duke of York, brother of Charles II. York supported Penn's petition for "a holy experiment" where people of all faiths might live in peace; and on March 4, 1681, Charles II approved the charter making Penn proprietor and governor of Pennsylvania. A year later, Penn received the "Lower Counties" which ultimately became Delaware. In his negotiations with the third Lord Baltimore over the Maryland-Pennsylvania boundary, the argument was similar to the 1631 dispute between the second Lord Baltimore and Claiborne—except that the royal commissioners who had rejected Claiborne now favored Penn. Yet Penn's claim that the disputed territory was *not uncultivated land inhabited only by savages* was exactly what Claiborne had said in justifying his right to Kent and the other Chesapeake islands he had settled prior to the 1634 arrival of the Marylanders. Thus, wrote Andrews, "if the latter opinion was just, the former was unjust, or *vice versa.*" Actually, nearly ninety years would lapse before the Maryland and Pennsylvania boundary was fixed permanently with surveys conducted by Charles Mason and Jeremiah Dixon.

Maryland became a crown colony in 1689, when its Catholic-dominated government was overthrown by Protestants who captured the statehouse and petitioned the crown to revoke the Calvert charter. In persistent appeals to friends at court to pressure the king's council to restore his province, Baltimore was unable to overcome his Catholic faith. In 1694, with Protestants firmly in control, Maryland's capital was moved from St. Mary's to Providence, which changed its name to Annapolis.

On February 21, 1715, Charles's son Benedict Leonard Calvert became the fourth Lord Baltimore. Because he had become a convert to the Church of England, he was hopeful that the Catholic problem would no longer stand as a barrier to his family's proprietorship of Maryland. But he died before any action could be taken.

The fifth Lord Baltimore, also named Charles, followed his father's lead in rejecting the old faith and soon enjoyed the full powers and privileges granted in the original Maryland charter. It was he who founded the city of Baltimore and, to the displeasure of his heir, lost nearly three million acres to Pennsylvania.

With Frederick Calvert, sixth Lord Baltimore, the noble line ended in disgrace. Described by Maryland historian W. H. Browne as "selfish, disreputable, dissolute, and degenerate," Frederick was interested in Maryland only to the extent the province financed his pleasures. The shame he brought to the Baltimore name was described in 1826 by John Burke in *A Genealogical and Heraldic History of the Peerage and Baronetage of the United Kingdom:*

> On February 12, 1768, Lord Baltimore was "brought up by habeas corpus before Lord Mansfield in the Court of Kings Bench ... as being charged upon the oath of Sarah Woodcock ... with having feloniously ravished and carnally known her against her will and consent." Charged with "having feloniously assisted, aided, and abetted him in the rape" were Anne Darby and Elizabeth

Grieffenburgh, but later it was found that the women were not present at the rape and their charge was reduced to "accessory before the fact."

Nothing more was reported on the matter.

The Lord Baltimore title died with Frederick Calvert in April 1771, and the proprietorship of Maryland was left to Henry Harford, his illegitimate son.

In 1675 Governor Berkeley, having been instructed by the crown to rebuild friendly relations with the Indians, refused to act when they assaulted Virginian's frontier settlements along the Potomac. As a result, Berkeley was accused by the frontiersmen of placating the Indians in order to protect his own profitable beaver trade and the holdings of the "Tidewater aristocracy" who acquired their land through his patronage. As the raids continued, a band of Virginia and Maryland vigilantes, under command of Colonel John Washington (ancestor of the first U.S. president), attacked a friendly tribe of Susquehannocks, ignoring their charge that the Seneca (a branch of the Iroquois) were to blame. Suddenly, border raids turned into all-out war, as the Susquehannocks joined with other Algonquian tribes to slaughter colonists from the Potomac to the James.

The frontier settlers, crying for help after being driven from their homes, found a leader in young Nathaniel Bacon, an aristocrat who raised an army of four hundred and marched against the Indians. When Bacon refused Berkeley's request to disband, the governor proclaimed him a rebel. Hence, Bacon's Rebellion, or Revolution, as Stephen Saunders Webb called the outbreak of 1676 because it became a revolt "against dependence on England"—one in which revolutionaries took over the government of Virginia and seized the property of former officials admonished as "Traytors to the People." The announced goal of the rebels was to establish a popular government, whereby the governor as well as the legislators would be elected.

In opposition to the governor, the assembly declared war on the hostile Indians, commissioned Bacon a general and told him to increase the strength of his army through volunteers. Berkeley's response was to dissolve the assembly and accuse Bacon of treason, as the rebels set about destroying Indian villages throughout the colony and plundering the plantations of those Virginians who stood by the governor. Ultimately, they drove Berkeley into hiding and burned Jamestown. And before it was over, wrote Webb, the rebellion (or revolution) had "cost more lives, in proportion to population, than any other war in American history."

The fighting ended as quickly as it had started, when Bacon became ill with dysentery and died in October 1676. But the dying did not stop with the war's end. A vengeful Berkeley was determined "to convince the Country that wee are come to condeme and Punish."

In addition to charges of insurrection, Bacon was accused of trying to pressure sympathizers in Virginia, Maryland, and Carolina to support a scheme to secede from England in a move for independence. Berkeley confiscated the estates of at least twenty of Bacon's gentlemen followers and swore to hang as many as his troops could capture. That finally the governor's vengeance was held in check was due in large measure to Claiborne's son William and other peacemakers who served as members of the governor's court-martial.

A royal commission, following an investigation of the events which had caused so much death and ruin, pardoned most Bacon supporters and replaced Governor Berkeley.

In his "revisionist examination" of Bacon's Rebellion, Webb held that Virginia and the other colonies lost their political autonomy "for a century to come" as a consequence of the war. That may be so, but the crown did initiate colonial reforms which would no longer permit a royal governor to exercise the kind of dictatorial control enjoyed by Berkeley.

During the rebellion, the Claibornes were loyal to Governor Berkeley and his defense of the king's government. According to the commissioners' report, "Col. Wm. Claiborne, the Elder, and his sonnes were all of them Reported to us under character of Loyalty, and obedience to his Majesties Government and Losers both in stock and other Goods." The eldest son was singled out for his command of a fort at New Kent's Indiantown Landing, and for his influence in tempering Governor Berkeley's revenge against Bacon's followers.

Though Claiborne never returned to Kent or his other islands in the Chesapeake following the collapse of the Commonwealth and restoration of the English monarchy, he never forgot them. Even in his seventy-seventh year he made one more attempt to regain his territory and restore Virginia's traditional control of the bay. The timing seemed right when the royal commission was in Virginia monitoring the political aftermath of Bacon's Rebellion. Aware of the commission's concern that the proprietary entitlements of Maryland and North Carolina were undermining the king's interests in Virginia, and its suggestion that Charles II take control of both governments, Claiborne saw a good opportunity to restate his claim. In March 1677 he wrote to "his Majesties Commissioners for the Settlement of Virginia in these troublesome times of Rebellion and General disturbances":

The humble Representation of the Collony and Assembly of Virginia Shewing:

That all the time since the dissolution of the Virginia Patent not only then but ever since they have from time to time received assurances under the Broad Seale of England and by many other ways and declarations from the then King and ever since from time to time that their estates should bee in all respects conserved and in noe sort prejudiced. During which time the Petitioner Coll Claiborne hath been resident in Virginia and enjoyed as a Councellor and Secretary of State there the benefits thereof and did accordingly by virtue of Commissions under his Majesties Government and Seale of Virginia and by expressed directions from the Commissions under the Broad Seale of England discover and plant the Ile of Kent.

From time to time it continued under the Government of Virginia, warrants were directed to arrest men at the Ile of Kent; one man was brought down and tried in Virginia for felony and many were arrested for debt and returned to appear at James Citty; and so in many particulars.

It continued under the Government of Virginia untill Lord Baltamores officers came and expelled us by force of armed men severall times, but especially they wounded and then hanged our men without any tryall of Law, or any just cause given; they took away all our goods, servants and Catle there and in like maner they displanted us att Palmers Iland out of their lymits in Susquohanouh River: All this they did to us though we presented them and gave them Copies of his Majesties commands to the contrary, strictly commanding them not to molest us to which wee had noe other answer, than slighting and contempt.

Claiborne included copies of documents related to his case, along with this petition to "the Kings Most Excellent Majestie":

The humble Petition of Coll: Wm Claiborne, a Poore old servant of Your Majesties Father and Grandfather, Most Humbly Showeth,

That your Petitioner being one of the Councell of State to Your Majesties Grandfather: and after also Secretary of State to your Father of Glorious Memory: by these Speciall Commands under the

Broad Seale of England unto the Governour of Virginia By whome hee was sent out to discover & gaine a great trade of Beavers & furrs which the Duch Nation then usurped to themselves: And accordingly the Petitioner att his owne charge and in his owne person performed & to that purpose discovered & planted the Ile of Kent: & the Bay of Chesepeack which then well succeeding: The Old Lord Baltamore takeing notice thereof: Provided a Patent for the same ... Pretending it was unplanted and since by force of armes in a Hostile maner though forbidden by the then King: expelled the Petitioner and taking away his Estate to the value of above Ten thousand pounds sterling in Goods Catle Servants & many Plantations thereon which the Grand Assembly of Virginia hath lately instanced and presented to your Majestie as a great grievance of the Country: and hath been neare the utter undoeing of your Petitioner & family now in his old age: His younger yeares being most spent in his Discoveries & warrs against the Indians as Chiefe Comander.

Wherefore your Petitioner Humbly prostrates himself att your Majesties feet for speedy justice in so Lamentable a case and hee shall ever Pray.

Claiborne's appeal was endorsed by the Virginia assembly, which confirmed the timeworn complaint that "The Iland of Kent in Maryland, granted to, settled and planted by Colonel Claiborne, Senior, formerly a limb and member of Virginia (as may appear in our records, they having sent delegates to this Assembly, and divers other Indian proofs and evidence), is since lopped off and detained by Lord Baltimore."

The commissioners, also in sympathy with Claiborne's claim, wrote their own report:

This Petition of William Claiborne Senior being presented to us for a Grievance to be laid before his Majesties Royall Consideration, wee have accordingly here given in the same separately and by itself, as an affaire which concernes a whole peculiar Province, and which has heretofore beene before his Majesties Royal Father (of blessed memory) and most honorable Councill: without any decision being made thereon, is now again most humbly tendered to his Majestie to determine thereof according to his Royall wisdome, and to remaine under consideration till such time as the persons concerned, or some sent over hither by and from the Petitioners shall arrive to negotiate the same in England, which wee are not impowered or concerned to doe.

But no action was taken on his behalf. Thus, wrote Hale, when William Claiborne died before the year was out, his petition was, "with a suppressed sigh of relief conveniently tucked away by the King's Councillors."

It is believed that William Claiborne was buried at the old graveyard at Romancoke, the family seat near West Point where the York splits into the Pamunkey and Mattaponi Rivers. When the third Lord Baltimore learned that Claiborne had died in 1677, he was supposed to have said that "twas my indescribable pleasure ... to hear of the scoundrels death in Virginia."

Ownership of Romancoke exchanged hands on numerous occasions through the years. In 1795 it was controlled by George Washington who conveyed the estate to his nephew, George Washington Parke Custis. In 1857 Custis left Romancoke to his youngest grandson, Robert E. Lee, Jr., and it remained in Lee's possession until his death in 1914.

In 1680 Elizabeth Claiborne sold some of the family property. A large tract in Elizabeth City County was purchased by Thomas Jarvis, a successful merchant and sea captain who had married the widow of Nathaniel Bacon. That same year, in response to the Virginia governor's directive to establish new trade centers, the general assembly condemned fifty-acre sites for port towns on at least one major river in each of the counties; the land was to be vested in trustees and divided into half-acre lots. The port for Elizabeth City County was established on fifty acres of the Jarvis property along the Southampton River. When it was incorporated as Hampton in 1691, the name of Southampton River was abbreviated and the adjacent harbor became Hampton Roads. Located on the ancient Kecoughtan site where William Claiborne established his original Chesapeake Bay trading post in 1624, the old town emerged in the 1700s as "a place of the greatest trade in all Virginia." Today it is recognized as the oldest English speaking community in continuous existence outside the British Isles.

But what happened to William Claiborne's properties in the upper Chesapeake?

Palmer's Island, the small rock formation in the mouth of the Susquehanna River (where the proud Susquehannocks, their breasts decorated with images of animals and their arms laden with beaver pelts, offered to trade with the only Englishman they ever trusted) is now neglected and all but forgotten in its function as an anchor for the interstate connecting Baltimore and Philadelphia.

Poplar Island was given by Claiborne to his cousin Richard Thompson, whose family was killed there in 1637 by the Nanticoke Indians. The island was sold in 1654 for ten thousand pounds of tobacco to a Thomas Hawkins, sold again in 1699 to the former Dutch governor of Delaware, and eventually to the father of Charles Carroll, a signer of the Declaration of Independence. The British plundered Poplar Island in the War of 1812. Frederick Douglass, in his autobiography, recalled the days he had lived as a slave within view of the island, "covered with a thick, black pine forest." For Franklin Roosevelt and Harry Truman it was a presidential retreat. The victim of the bay's relentless erosion, Poplar has become a chain of ghostly islets sinking "inexorably into a watery grave," wrote Meyer. Once vital in human activity, it now is inhabited only by birds and a few deer.

Kent Island, north of Poplar Island and east of Annapolis, is linked to Maryland's western shore by the Chesapeake Bay Bridge. Today, the busy island is proud to claim recognition as "The First English Settlement Within Maryland," and many inhabitants look upon William Claiborne as a sort of folk hero. But nowhere is there a plaque or statue commemorating the man who established the settlement in 1631, although his name shows up from time to time in a Claiborne Road or Claiborne's Landing. A village of attractive homes retains the name of the Romancoke plantation, and the site of the Crayford plantation is now Crafford.

In 1994 a team of weekend archeologists claimed they turned up evidence of Claiborne's fort and trading post inside the remains of an ancient barrel well buried in the mud flats forty feet from Kent Island's southern shoreline. According to a Baltimore newspaper account, they found a few trading beads "and a small brass straight pin of a type listed in inventories of the stock at Claiborne's trading post." Though the site is yet to be authenticated, the chief archeologist for the Maryland Historical Trust believed the findings showed that the old Kent Island fort is now under water.

The only "official" recognition of Claiborne's impact on the early days of the colony appeared in an article in the September 1912 issue of the *Maryland Historical Magazine*. Under the headline, "Chief Executive Officers of Maryland During The Provincial Period," the first name on the list was that of "William Claiborne, [who] under a trading commission dated May 16, 1631, settled at Kent Island August 17, 1631, and governed it under authority of Virginia." The second name on the list was that of "Leonard Calvert, commissioned [Deputy

Governor in 1633] by his brother, Cecilius Calvert, second Lord Baltimore and first Lord Proprietor of Maryland."

The Claiborne name also survives on the Maryland map in a tiny village on the Eastern Shore, just nine miles from picturesque St. Michael's. Once the home of the Jefferson Island Club, a political rendezvous frequented by presidents and lesser Democrats, it is now described as a spit of land "almost washed away by the tides." In 1886 Claiborne was the terminus of the Baltimore & Eastern Shore Railroad, chartered by General Joseph B. Seth to run from Broad Cove on "Eastern Bay" to the Ocean City beaches. Seth wrote: "I have long been an admirer of William Claiborne and have felt that he was unjustly treated by the Maryland Colony. He had a perfectly legal grant from the Virginia Colony and ... ought not to have been disturbed. Maryland has made no effort to commemorate his name." Seth continued: "This terminus of the road on Eastern Bay was directly across from Kent Island and the adjoining property known as Wade's Point, so I concluded to name that station, which I was sure would grow into a Town, as it has, Claiborne." And he named his first steamer *William Claiborne*, for the man who "had been unjustly treated and who, from his whole record, showed that he was a man of force and strong character."

Even the ferry allusion has some interest. In colonial days, transportation in the Chesapeake region was dependent upon a series of ferries on both sides of the bay, when the only function of many of the roads was to connect one ferry with another. Though Maryland was more successful than Virginia in establishing free ferries, on occasion one of the Lords Baltimore would seek control over the ferries with the intent of increasing his proprietary revenues. In the mid-1700s there were a number of ferries making regular runs between Kent Island and Annapolis in one direction and Kent Island and the Eastern Shore in the other, some of which were operated by women; notably one Jane Claiborne.

Thus the Claiborne name has lived on also in legend and the deeds of descendants. One son died a hero in a 1684 Indian uprising and was buried at Romancoke. The descendant William C. C. Claiborne helped frame the constitution of Tennessee and served as the territorial governor of Louisiana, which in 1812 was the first territory admitted to the United States. Another descendant assisted Andrew Jackson in planning the Battle of New Orleans. One, a major-general in the Confederate army, was known as the "Stonewall of the West." A

Claiborne married the uncle of President William Henry Harrison, others were related by marriage to governors of Virginia, New York, and Massachusetts, and Claiborne descendants have served as United States congressmen from at least five states.

The Lords Baltimore are remembered in Maryland in the names of Calvert and Baltimore Counties and also in the state's largest city located on the Patapsco River, an arm of the Chesapeake. Chartered in 1729 as a tobacco port, the city of Baltimore is today one of the major shipping centers, and ranks among the top three American ports in the volume of foreign trade handled.

John Herbert Claiborne wrote that Cecil Calvert and William Claiborne "were well matched in tenacity of purpose, persistence, cleverness and resource, but [Calvert] was a Prince of Principalities with power behind him and Claiborne was a simple gentleman with only his ability, his courage, and the friends he made. That Baltimore won and Claiborne lost may be explained partly on geographic lines and partly on the differences in their status. In the nature of things, Kent Island had to fall to Baltimore by reason of its geographical position but that does not influence the question of the moral and abstract right involved."

Oswald Tilghman, in his *History of Talbot County, Maryland, 1661-1861*, said this about Maryland's first European settler: "William Claiborne has been hardly dealt with, not only by the early provincial authorities [who] deprived him of his rights and property, but by the annalists and historians [who] have attempted to deprive him of his good name." Tilghman felt it was difficult to arrive at an accurate concept of Claiborne's character and temper, because so many of the accounts "have been transmitted to us by writers who seem to have no end in view but to lavish upon him the most opprobrious epithets." Andrews expanded on this sentiment to reprimand writers on both sides of the Chesapeake conflict: "It is unfortunate that sundry Virginia writers, through the past two hundred years, should have seen fit to abuse Cecil Calvert whilst praising the courage and determination of Claiborne to stand by his claims .... It seems equally unfortunate that so many Maryland historians have felt it incumbent upon them to cast the sharpest animadversions upon Captain Claiborne as a turncoat without fixed convictions."

The Marylander John H. B. Latrobe thought it difficult to believe that Claiborne "had not a better claim, and was not a better and truer man, than historians, thus far, have been willing to admit."

Epilogue

*"Then there's hope a great man's memory
may outlive his life half a year."*

Or so wrote Shakespeare.

Still, wrote Latrobe in 1854, the time will come when William Claiborne's "memory will be relieved from the imputations of contemporary partisans, and when he will be recognized as the brave soldier, the gallant gentlemen, acute in council, whom danger could not turn aside nor defeat dishearten—the statesman of the wilderness, the attainted of the proprietary government, only to become, in turn, the commissioner of the Commonwealth of England, to subjugate the province, from which he had been driven as a rebel; and who ... whether in power or out of power, exercised an influence, or inspired a dread, due alone [said McMahon's *History of Maryland*] to 'his unceasing efforts to maintain, by courage and address, the territory which his enterprise had discovered and planted.'"

History seems to be on Shakespeare's side. Perhaps the best that William Claiborne's memory can hope to inspire at this late date is the ballad written by Folger McKinsey some eighty or ninety years ago. For a period of forty-two years (1906-1948), McKinsey wrote a column for *The Baltimore Sun* newspaper which he signed "The Bentztown Bard." An early column was devoted to the ballad that sang of an age in "sweet Maryland" when "swords rang together in valour's rude chime" and swart Claiborne of Kent "prayed like a Roundhead and fought like a rogue!"

Hi-dando, di-dando! Blow, bugles of Kent!
Of all the fine gentlemen heav'n ever sent,
Here's ruddy, swart Claiborne, the finest and best,
With lace at his wristbands and war in his breast—
A faithful Anglican, when kings were in vogue,
Who prayed like a Roundhead and fought like a rogue!

Hi-dando, di-dando! Hurray for the day
That walks like a glory across the blue bay!
What leaping of hearts when the blunderbus roars!
What bending of backs to the stroke of the oars!
Blow, bugles of battle, the morning is sweet.
Though the sun may set red in the blood of defeat!

Hi-dando, di-dando! They've fought; they have lost!
With Claiborne afar, and the slow barges tost
On tides that will never return them with those
Who kissed in the dawn the red lips of each rose
That leaned in her love, with "Good-by, and come home
From the rain of the battle, the roar of the foam!"

Hi-dando, di-dando! With Kent for his zone,
He'll make the King's Maryland the King's and his own!
Though lost be the battle, the chief will survive
To argue and parley and scheme and connive,
And win a brief triumph, to fade through the years,
With the Calverts deposed and sweet Maryland in tears!

Hi-dando, di-dando! The barges have gone
Like phantoms of mist on the ripples of dawn,
And sweethearts and daughters who bade them adieu
And under the roses, sweet Kentland, of you!
The logs of your cabins, old settlers, are strewn
In the mold of the forest from which they were hewn!

Hi-dando, di-dando! Swart men of the time
When swords rang together in valour's rude chime;
Brave leaders, stanch liegemen, have gone in their glee
From the councils of courage beneath the oak tree—
But Kent blooms in glory all down her sweet length
Because of their high-hearted spirit and strength!

Hi-dando, di-dando! No sound in the morn
Of bugles, except the glad ring of the horn
The hunters sound gayly across the fair glen
To summon the hounds and the merry young men,
And waken the shadows with notes that have fled
With the songs of the bargemen on lips that are dead!

Hi-dando, di-dando! Wake, Kentland, and sing!
He found you, and lost you; but, oh, when the spring
Sweeps sweet through your orchards, in gladness we call
Because, in your beauty, he found you at all,
And named you, and loved you, and left you to lie
A garden of glory full-ripe to the sky!

Hi-dando, di-dando! His dust is afar
On the hills of the dawn and the vales of the star;
The battles are over, the bugles at rest,
The dream of sweet peace folds its wings o'er his breast:
For the Church, and the King, and the good that he meant
Let the red roses blossom for Claiborne of Kent!

William Claiborne and the Lords Baltimore battled for control of the upper Chesapeake for half a century. Though their war ended with Claiborne's death in 1677, border disputes and quarrels between Maryland and Virginia over Chesapeake Bay fishing and oyster rights did not.

The two states agreed to a compact in 1785 preserving their access to waters that formed their common boundary, but Virginia continued to pass laws to protect its oyster interests. An act in 1832 denied Maryland's oyster rights in Accomack and Northampton Counties (located on Virginia's Eastern Shore). In 1867 the Virginia assembly declared that "no persons, other than a citizen of this state, shall catch terrapins or clams, catch, take or plant oysters in the Rivers Pocomoke or Potomac." Virginia captured so many violators and confiscated so many vessels that Marylanders claimed they were "threatened with starvation." As a result, the Virginia law was modified in 1872, allowing Maryland citizens access to oysters in the Pocomoke and Potomac but denying them "the right to catch, take or plant oysters in any creek, cove, or inlet tributary to said rivers."

In 1877 a board of arbitration redefined the Maryland-Virginia boundary and gave the Potomac River to Maryland. But Virginia still denied Marylanders the right to take oysters in Tangier or Pocomoke Sounds. The Virginia law made a major distinction between Pocomoke Sound and Pocomoke River (where in 1635 William Claiborne's sloop, the *Cockatrice*, encountered two of Lord Baltimore's vessels, the *St. Helen* and *St. Margaret*, in the first naval conflict in American waters). Pocomoke River originates in the Great Cypress Swamp on the Maryland-Delaware border, winds its way through Maryland, and empties into Pocomoke Sound at Cheapeake Bay, close to the line separating Maryland and Virginia.

Commissioners appointed by the two states tried to settle the dispute at a meeting held at Point Comfort, Virginia, in 1890. They failed when "other complications arose." Louis Whealton described those complications in his 1897 dissertation on *The Maryland and Virginia Boundary Controversy:*

> *The oyster beds of the Chesapeake and its tributaries had increased rapidly in value, and Virginia protected her interests in this industry as she had never done before. Marylanders who ventured over the line of 1877 to take oysters ran the risk of being captured by the Virginia authorities. In April of 1890, the Maryland General Assembly passed an act which authorized the Attorney-General of the State "to take such steps as may be necessary and proper to obtain as soon as possible a decision of the Supreme Court of the United States as to the scope and effect of the compact of 1785 ... whether or not it applies to that body of water now called 'Pocomoke Sound,' through which the boundary line between Maryland and Virginia now passes, and whether or not the citizens of Maryland have a right to take oysters in said water jointly with the citizens of the State of Virginia, a right which the citizens of Maryland have enjoyed from the date of 'said compact' until about the year 1883, without molestation."*

Before the court decision, Virginia authorities were at war with Maryland oystermen who had crossed the line to take advantage of the greater yield of Virginia's oyster beds. The state was "at the mercy of these marauders," announced the Virginia governor. He added: "We are powerless to defend our rights, and daily and hourly these desperate men are found in our waters plying their vocation and carrying away the property of the state which she has declared shall be preserved for the use of her own citizens."

Guns were heard in Tangier Sound on February 27, 1894. Wrote Whealton: "Eight or ten Maryland boats were found at work on the Virginia side of the dividing line and they were fired upon by the Virginia steamer *Chesapeake* of the oyster fleet. The Marylanders fled, returning fire, and were pursued into Maryland and arrested. Hardly had the news of this episode become generally known before Governor Brown, of Maryland, in response to a telegram, despatched the steamer *Governor Thomas* armed with a breech loading cannon and breech loading rifles to the Annamessex River [north of Pocomoke

Sound]. This time the trouble was with the Virginia dredgers, illegally taking oysters."

Whealton noted that "the question as to whether one State could lawfully seize the vessels of the other when once they had passed into their native waters" was addressed by the Virginia assembly. An act was passed "to provide for reciprocal rights and powers" and ruled that "the offender can be pursued by the legally constituted authorities of said state whether the offense was committed up to and across the boundary line between said states, into the said waters of said state where the offender resides, to a distance not exceeding ten miles." Maryland passed a similar act.

On April 23, 1894, the United States Supreme Court defined the fishing rights of Maryland and declared Pocomoke Sound separate and distinct from Pocomoke River. The court decided that the compact of 1785 between Maryland and Virginia gave "no right to citizens of Maryland to fish or take oysters in the waters of Pocomoke Sound."

Though the violence has been tempered, the border dispute has continued up to the present day.

BIBLIOGRAPHY

Adams, Robert M. *The Land and Literature of England.* Norton, 1983.

Andrews, Matthew Page. *Virginia the Old Dominion.* Doubleday, 1937.

Andrews, Matthew Page. *The Founding of Maryland.* Williams & Wilkins, 1933.

Archives of Maryland, *Proceedings and Acts of the General Assembly of Maryland, 1637/8-1664*, Edited by William Hand Browne. Published by the Authority of the State Under the Direction of the Maryland Historical Society, 1883.

Ashley, Maurice. *England in the Seventeenth Century 1603-1714.* Penguin, 1962.

Barth, John. *The Sot-Weed Factor.* Doubleday, 1960.

Brinton, Crane, John B. Christopher, and Robert L. Wolff. *A History of the Last Five Centuries.* Edited by Donald C. McKay. Prentiss-Hall, 1957.

Campbell, Charles. *History of the Colony and Ancient Dominion of Virginia.* Lippincott, 1860.

Captain John Smith's Map of New England (1623), with Changes Added Between 1624 and 1631.

Carmer, Carl. *The Susquehanna.* Rinehart, 1955.

Carlton, Charles. *Charles I: The Personal Monarch.* ARK, 1984.

Chapman, Blanche Adams. *Wills and Administrations of Elizabeth City County, Virginia 1688-1800.* Genealogical Publishing Co., Inc., 1980.

Churchill, Winston. *A History of the English Speaking People*. Dodd, Mead, 1956.

Claiborne, John Herbert. *William Claiborne of Virginia*. Putnam, 1917.

Colley, Linda. *Britons*. Yale University Press, 1992.

Encyclopedia Americana, International Edition. Grolier, 1989.

The New Encyclopaedia Britannica. Vol. 3, 1985.

Encyclopedia International. Lexicon, 1981.

Fodor's *Chesapeake*. Fodor's Travel Publications Inc., 1986.

Hale, Nathaniel C. *Virginia Venturer, a Historical Biography of William Claiborne, 1600-1677*. Dietz Press, 1951.

Hall, Clayton Colman, ed. *Narratives of Early Maryland 1633-1684*. Scribner's, 1910.

Harris, Malcolm H., compiler. *Old New Kent County: Some Accounts of the Planters, Plantations, and Places in New Kent County, Vol. I*. Copyrighted 1977.

Harrison, Fairfax. *Virginia Land Grants*. Old Dominion, 1925.

History of Mason and Dixon's Line. Contained in an Address by John H. B. Latrobe of Maryland, to the Pennsylvania Historical Society, November 8, 1854.

Johnson, Allen, and Dumas Malone, editors. *Dictionary of American Biography, Vol. 2*. Scribner's, 1937.

Kavenagh, W. Keith. ed. *Foundations of Colonial America*. Chelsea House with R. R. Bowker, 1973.

Keatley, J. K. *Place Names of the Eastern Shore of Maryland*. Queen Anne Press, 1987.

Kenny, Hamill. *The Place Names of Maryland, Their Origin and Meaning*. Maryland Historical Society, 1984.

MacDonald, William, ed. *Documentary Source Book of American History*. MacMillan, 1908.

Marshall, John. Introduction to *Life of Washington*. 5 volumes, Fredericksburg edition, 1916.

Meyer, Eugene L. *Maryland Lost and Found*. Johns Hopkins Press, 1986.

Meyer, Eugene L. *Chesapeake Country*. Abbeville Press, 1990.

Middleton, Albert Pierce. *Tobacco Coast, A Maritime History of Chesapeake Bay in the Colonial Era*. Johns Hopkins Press, 1984.

Morison, Samuel Eliot. *Oxford History of the American People*. Oxford, 1965.

Morris, Richard B. *Encyclopedia of American History*. Harper, 1953.

Old Kecoughtan. William and Mary College Quarterly Historical Magazine, Series 1, Vol. 9, No. 2, 1901.

Semmes, Ralph. *Captains and Mariners of Early Maryland*. Johns Hopkins Press, 1937.

Smith, Captain John. *The Generall Historie of Virginia, The Fourth Booke*. 1624.

Shomette, Donald G. *Pirates on the Chesapeake*. Tidewater, 1985.

Skirven, Percy C. *The First Parishes of the Province of Maryland*. Norman, Remington, 1923.

Strachey, William. *Historie of Travaile into Virginia Britannia*. Reprinted from Original 1612 Manuscript by Hakluyt Society, 1849.

Torrence, Clayton. *The English Ancestry of William Claiborne of Virginia*. The Virginia Magazine of History and Biography, Vol. 56, No. 3-4, 1948.

Tyler, Lyon G. *England in America*. Cooper Square, 1968.

Tyler, Lyon G., compiler. *History of Hampton and Elizabeth City County, Virginia*. 1912.

Voynick, Stephen M. *The Mid-Atlantic Treasure Coast*. Middle Atlantic Press, 1984.

Webb, Stephen Saunders. *1676 The End of American Independence*. Knopf, 1994.

Wheaton, Louis N. *The Maryland and Virginia Boundary Controversy (1668-1894)*. A Dissertation Presented to the Board of University Studies of the Johns Hopkins University, June 1897.

Whitelaw, Ralph T. *Virginia's Eastern Shore: A History of Northampton and Accomack Counties*. Copyright 1951 by the Virginia Historical Society.

Williamson, Gene. *Of the Sea and Skies*. Heritage Books, Inc., 1993.

Yong, Captain Thomas. 1634 Letter Quoted in *Narratives of Early Maryland 1633-1684*. Original in Virginia State Library.

INDEX

Names, Places, and Events

www.ingramcontent.com/pod-product-compliance
Lightning Source LLC
Chambersburg PA
CBHW070450090426
42735CB00012B/2501

9 780788 403309